THRINADH SAI

FROM SILENCE TO DIALOGUE

A Path to Collective Wisdom

First edition

This book was professionally typeset on Reedsy.
Find out more at reedsy.com

"You can't cross the sea merely by standing and staring at the water."

Rabindranath Tagore

Contents

Preface iii
Prologue v

I Early Roots of Moral Inquiry

1 A House Full of Echoes 3
2 Unsteady Foundations 11

II Seeking Understanding Amid Complexity

3 A World Without Anchors 23
4 Small Steps Toward the Light 34

III Finding a Voice and Purpose

5 Shaping a Voice of My Own 51
6 Embracing the Wider Horizon 62

IV Integration Moral Reasoning into Adult Life

7 Walking Into the Wider World 71
8 Expanding the Circle of Influence 87

V Consolidating Moral Traditions

9 Weaving Morality into the Tapestry of Daily Life 105
10 Passing the Torch of Moral Reasoning 117

VI Ensuring the Practice Endures

11 A Legacy of Moral Inquiry 133
12 The Tapestry Unfurls Beyond a Lifetime 146

Epilogue 153
References and Resources 155
Behind the Dialogue 160
About the Author 163

Preface

Before you begin the journey through these chapters, allow me to set the stage for what you're about to encounter. This is not a conventional self-help book, nor is it a purely academic exploration of psychology and philosophy. Instead, think of it as a conversation between my personal life story and the broader human narrative we all share. It's a meeting place of memory and research, of deeply personal confessions and universal truths.

As I wrote, I kept two images in mind. One was the frightened child I used to be—curled up in the corner of a small room, confused by the cruelty around him. The other was the curious adult I have become—sitting quietly at a desk, surrounded by books, determined to understand why people behave the way they do, and how we can break free from patterns that harm us.

In the pages that follow, you'll read about violence and fear, about misguided habits and moral confusion. You'll also see how, in spite of it all, it's possible to grow toward something brighter. Philosophy and psychology became my guides, showing me how the mind is molded by forces both intimate and global: family trauma, cultural pressures, personal choices, and learned responses. They helped me see that I am not alone in my struggles; the patterns I found in my life exist in other lives too. By studying these patterns, we can learn a great deal about ourselves and each other.

I invite you to approach this book with an open heart. These stories and insights are offered so we can recognize our shared humanity—the pain and the promise within every individual mind. My hope is that readers will not only find echoes of their own experiences here, but also come away with a deeper understanding of what it means to be human: fragile, resilient, capable of error, yet always able to learn and heal.

Let us walk this path together, as companions exploring new territories. May this atlas serve as your guide to understanding how we are shaped—and how we might reshape ourselves into something more compassionate, self-aware, and free.

Prologue

I remember the silence between screams. It's strange how, as a child, you can stand in the corner of a tiny room and still feel as if the world has shrunk to the size of your own trembling heart. I can see myself there, watching my parents fight, afraid to move, afraid to cry, afraid to exist. Back then, I believed fear was the only map I had—each bruise, each shouted insult marking another dark territory in my mind.

Today, I stand in a different place. I'm older, but those shadows are still with me. They whisper through old memories, reminding me how a life can be shaped by violence, by silence, and by things no one ever bothered to explain. Yet, I'm here now, writing this, determined to understand my own story and share it so that others might find their way out of the darkness that once trapped me.

This book is my attempt to chart the hidden landscapes of the mind—not just my own, but the mind we all share. It's a journey guided by the echoes of childhood trauma, the quiet desperation of adolescence, and the revelations that emerged when I discovered philosophy, literature, and psychology. I will show you how my personal struggles connect to the universal struggles of countless others, how the pain of a single life can reflect patterns of human behavior repeated across cultures and generations.

Think of these pages as an atlas, one that lays out emotional terrains shaped by family, society, addiction, abuse, and the slow, steady awakening of self-awareness. I've learned that we are not doomed to remain prisoners of our pasts. By understanding the psychology that molds us, we can reshape our inner worlds.

As I open this atlas and invite you in, I'm sharing not only my scars, but also the tools and truths that helped me heal. May you find in these words the courage to explore your own interior landscapes, to question old beliefs, and to discover the paths that lead from suffering to understanding, and from understanding to hope.

I

Early Roots of Moral Inquiry

1

A House Full of Echoes

I remember the sound of footsteps before I remember faces. As a small child, perhaps five or six years old, I learned to read the subtle changes in the rhythm of my father's steps as he approached the door. There was the slow shuffle that meant he had returned from a long day's work. There was the unsteady stomp and the thick smell of liquor that meant I should shrink into the corners of our single-room home. Our house in Chowduvada was modest—just a single room serving as kitchen, living area, and bedroom, with an outdoor bathroom. It was small enough that no one could truly hide, but large enough to echo the sounds of raised voices, sobs, and sometimes screams.

In those early years, my world was defined by the boundaries of that room and the immediate people around me: my mother, my father, my grandmother, and the absent figure of my grandfather who had died before I truly knew him. The story of my family's turmoil had, as I later understood, a lot to do with inheritance and disappointment. My grandfather, a government school assistant, had passed away, leaving behind the expectation that his job would go to my father. He had worked hard all his life, and in our community, it was not uncommon for a government job to pass to a family member upon one's death.

But my grandmother, widowed and afraid of losing financial security, decided that the job should go to my father's brother instead.

On paper, the reasoning was simple. My father, Venkata Ramana, had only studied until the seventh standard. His brother had completed the tenth. In the eyes of the officials and, perhaps, my grandmother's own judgment, the brother seemed more suitable for the position. But to my father, this was a betrayal—evidence that his own mother favored his younger brother and left him to struggle. Even though I was too young to grasp all the nuances, I could sense this tension. It simmered in the background, an unspoken grievance that would explode into arguments after a few drinks.

My earliest memories of fear and confusion come from witnessing how easily conversations turned into fights. My father, who worked as a lorry driver, often came home tired, frustrated, and, more frequently than not, drunk. When he entered our home after drinking, the atmosphere changed instantaneously. My mother, Sujatha, would stiffen. My grandmother, Sitaratnam, might retreat quietly to a corner, feigning busyness. And I would simply become very small—pressing myself against the wall or trying to vanish behind a piece of furniture.

Psychologists have long studied the effects of domestic violence and unstable home environments on children. Research suggests that in households fraught with conflict, children develop heightened sensitivity to changes in tone of voice, footsteps, and facial expressions. They learn, before they even know the word "trauma," that the world can become dangerous without warning. According to attachment theory, proposed by John Bowlby and expanded by Mary Ainsworth, the quality of early parent-child bonds sets the stage for how a child will view relationships and trust others. In my case, I learned that adults were unpredictable. Love might be present, but it was buried under layers of anger and unmet expectations.

There were times my father would demand money from my mother for alcohol. She had none to give—she, who carried gas cylinders up steep hills for a few rupees, who stretched every bit of her earnings to feed us. When she refused, he would lash out. The sound of a slap, the dull thud of a kick against her body, the sobbing that followed—these sounds etched themselves into my mind. In those moments, I learned that disagreement could end in violence. It was an early lesson that safety was never guaranteed.

It's important to note that what I'm describing is not unique. Across the world, countless children wake up in homes where anger and uncertainty loom large. Studies from organizations like the World Health Organization and UNICEF highlight how domestic violence and parental substance abuse are global issues affecting millions of children. The details differ by region and culture, but the psychological imprint is similar: children learn about their place in the world from these early encounters. They may develop insecure attachment styles—anxious, avoidant, or even disorganized—because the very people who should provide security are sources of fear.

I recall one particularly vivid memory that stands out like a red thread in a tapestry of gray. It was a day when my mother, despite everything, was smiling. She was cooking, slicing vegetables, telling me some small story about our family's past. I must have been playing with a simple toy—perhaps a broken piece of plastic that I imagined was a car. Her voice was warm, and I remember feeling a calmness that was rare in our home. Suddenly, my father returned, drunkenly pushing the door open. He demanded money again, shouting abuses at my mother. She refused, her voice trembling but firm. I watched, heart pounding. He kicked her in the stomach. She hit the wall and fell unconscious.

In the silence that followed his departure, I found myself frozen. I didn't cry immediately; I think shock took over. Then I ran outside to call my maternal grandmother from the neighboring house. My grandmother rushed in, trying to revive my mother. Eventually, my mother came back to consciousness, sobbing and holding me close. This scene, tragic and intimate, is one I've relived in my mind countless times. In that moment, I knew that something was fundamentally wrong, but I had no words for it. Children often lack the vocabulary to articulate their trauma. They feel it physically—an ache in the chest, a knot in the stomach, trembling legs—but cannot name it. Psychologists call this inability "alexithymia," the difficulty in identifying and describing one's own emotions. While I wouldn't say I was alexithymic, I was certainly too young to say, "I am afraid," or "I feel helpless." Instead, I absorbed the fear into my bones.

As I grew slightly older—still just a boy, but a year or two on—I remember the hush that fell over my family when we moved to Visakhapatnam, trying to escape the chaos of Chowduvada. My mother hoped that leaving the village behind would free us from the cycles of violence. She believed, naively perhaps, that a change of scenery could heal old wounds. But psychological patterns run deeper than geography. My father's drinking continued, and the fights persisted. What changed was the scenery and the neighbors, but not the essence of our lives.

All the while, I was learning lessons about human interaction. I learned that adults sometimes hurt the people they should protect. I learned that shouting was a way to express power, and crying was a way to release pain. Nobody sat me down to explain right or wrong, cause and effect. Discipline was not instruction but punishment. Many developmental psychologists emphasize the importance of guidance—children need consistent explanations, emotional validation, and understanding to develop healthy moral compasses. In my environment, there was a profound lack of that. Mistakes were met with scolding or beatings, not with conversations. Over time, a child might internalize the idea that questions and vulnerability earn you pain, not understanding.

Even something as fundamental as going to school became complicated. Fear of authority, born in my home, extended to the school environment. I remember seeing latecomers at school being beaten by the teachers. This mirrored what I saw at home: the powerful asserting control through violence. Terrified, I ran away instead of entering the classroom. When I returned home, I found no one there to help me understand this fear. Running to my aunt's house didn't help either—she wasn't there. I was lost, literally and metaphorically. In that moment, the world felt like a maze of locked doors, no adult voice guiding me to safety. When I was eventually found and punished by my mother and the principal, it only reinforced the lesson: the world is harsh, punishment is inevitable, and no one asks why you're afraid. Children in such circumstances often develop what psychologists term "learned helplessness"—the feeling that no matter what you do, you cannot change the outcome, so you stop trying to resist or improve your situation.

This pattern of not being asked "why" is crucial. Part of healthy psychological development involves having caregivers who inquire about a child's inner world. "Why did you run away?" "What scared you?" Without such questions, a child might never learn to articulate fears or understand their own motivations. The result is an internal chaos that mirrors the external chaos. The child's view of the world becomes that of an unstable, threatening place where one's own feelings and needs are irrelevant.

In my own narrative, I see how easily I drifted into behaviors that perpetuated self-harm and confusion. Stealing money, avoiding school, seeking comfort in pornography—these were maladaptive coping mechanisms formed in an environment devoid of healthy guidance. It's no surprise that I gravitated toward immediate gratifications. When life offers you no stable ground, you clutch at whatever gives momentary relief. Research into childhood development shows that when basic emotional needs are not met, children often turn toward behaviors that stimulate short bursts of pleasure or control. The simple act of stealing money or indulging in secretive habits can feel like reclaiming a sense of power or pleasure in a world that offers none.

Yet, even as a child, I sensed there must be something else—some other way of living that didn't involve fear and violence. I think this sense of "something else" is a spark many children carry, even in dire circumstances. It might be innate human curiosity or a faint glimmer of hope. Developmental psychology suggests that children are wired for resilience. Given the right support, they can recover from hardships. But in my early years, that support was absent. Instead, I had my own silent observations. When I saw neighbors peacefully discussing problems, I felt a pang of envy. When I encountered teachers who spoke kindly to other students, I wondered what it would be like to trust adults.

If there is one universal thread to draw from these early memories, it's that countless children around the world grow up with similar emotional landscapes. The specifics vary—some face political violence, others endure extreme poverty or cultural oppression—but the psychological patterns share commonalities. Children interpret the world through interactions with their primary caregivers. When those caregivers are caught in cycles of addiction, violence, or despair, the child learns lessons of fear and uncertainty. This, in turn, can ripple out into adolescence and adulthood, influencing behavior, relationships, and self-perception for years to come.

Developmental psychologist Urie Bronfenbrenner spoke about the "ecological systems" in which a child grows. From the immediate family to the larger community and society, all these layers interact to shape a child's mind. In my story, the immediate system—my father's violence, my mother's helplessness, my grandmother's silence—was toxic. The broader community, which might have offered support, often remained passive spectators, occasionally providing gossip or moral judgment rather than meaningful intervention. The cultural norms around masculinity, alcohol, and family duty also played their part. It was a complex ecosystem that offered little emotional shelter.

Another concept to consider is the transmission of trauma across generations. Research in epigenetics and family systems therapy suggests that trauma can be passed down, not just psychologically but even biologically. It's possible that my father's rage was fueled by unresolved traumas of his own upbringing, and my mother's helplessness was shaped by societal constraints on women's power. Understanding these generational links can foster compassion, though it does not excuse violence or suffering. It merely illustrates that these patterns did not appear from nowhere. They were part of a larger human story—one in which individuals often struggle to break free from inherited burdens.

As I look back now, writing these words, I see that first chapter of my life as a blueprint for the mind I would carry into adolescence and early adulthood. Those early years taught me how fear can become second nature, how confusion can replace clarity, and how desperate one becomes for a moment of comfort, no matter how unhealthy it might be. Children's brains are exquisitely sensitive to their environments, and the "house full of echoes" I grew up in left its marks on my neural architecture. These marks influenced my reactions to stress, my interpretation of relationships, and my understanding of right and wrong.

But this chapter is not just about despair. It is also about planting the seeds of awareness. Even as a child, I was taking mental notes. I didn't know it then, but the confusion I felt would one day lead me to seek answers. The silence around my fears would push me toward books, knowledge, and the introspection that would come later. In that sense, trauma can sometimes be a dark teacher. It shows you what is lacking in your life—kindness, stability, understanding—so that later, if you ever find these things, you recognize their value.

By starting the book with these painful, personal memories, I invite readers to step into a world that may be unfamiliar or uncomfortably close to their own. This is the baseline: a frightened child in a corner, absorbing the chaos around him. Understanding the psychological impact of this starting point is the key to understanding everything that followed—my delinquent adolescence, my struggles with addiction and confusion, and eventually, my turn toward philosophy and psychology in a desperate attempt to make sense of it all.

In the chapters to come, we will leave this small room and travel through different phases of my life, and in doing so, we will touch upon universal patterns of human behavior, supported by research and theory. We will see how one child's fear can illuminate broader truths about our shared human condition. But for now, let this first chapter rest as it is: an honest, painful account of a house echoing with anger and fear, and a child listening, learning, and waiting for an explanation that would not come until many years later.

2

Unsteady Foundations

In the dim light of early morning, I awoke to the subtle sounds of a world that felt both familiar and foreign: the distant hum of industrial work from the HPCL plant where my maternal grandfather labored as a daily wage earner, the soft voices of neighbors chattering as they passed by, and the distant horns of buses and auto-rickshaws navigating the uneven roads of Sriharipuram. We had left the old village behind, the one with its cramped single-room house and my father's fury pounding through the walls, and settled near my maternal grandparents. Although the living space was still modest—a small cluster of rooms near the edge of a modest hillside—there was a slight, almost imperceptible shift. The home might have been simple, but it offered a relative calm that I had rarely known before.

My mother, Sujatha, moved us here in an attempt to escape the unrelenting violence that had defined our earlier existence. She believed, with the desperate hope of someone who has known only storms, that a change of place might bring forth a gentle drizzle instead of a hurricane. There were no guarantees. My father still drank. He still spent his income on alcohol, leaving her with nothing. Yet, in this new environment, my mother's parents—my grandfather, Kamunaidu, and my grandmother, Manga—provided a slender pillar of stability. They fed us, sheltered us, and offered a kind of quiet endurance. Sometimes that's enough, or so my mother must have thought.

It was in these days that I witnessed my mother's strength as much as her suffering. She carried heavy gas cylinders up a steep hill, receiving a few rupees—ten, twenty, thirty at most—for each delivery. She scrubbed floors and cleaned utensils in strangers' homes for a small wage. The labor was relentless, the pay meager, but she pressed on. In her face, I saw a tension that I couldn't name then: fear, despair, maybe a flicker of pride in managing to feed her child against all odds. Psychologists speak often of resilience, of how some individuals weather unimaginable hardships and still find the will to go on. My mother's resilience was a silent testament to that. She had neither the language of psychological theories nor the privilege of therapy sessions, but she carried on, day after day, as if muscle and bone alone could hold a shattered family upright.

Still, fear lingered in every corner. My father's absence was never guaranteed. His name hovered over our lives like a threat. Sometimes he would return unannounced, always intoxicated, always angry. He demanded money we did not have, accused my mother of conspiracies and neglect, blamed her for every misfortune that had ever befallen him. On one grim evening, I remember a time around nine or nine-thirty at night. We were all inside, finishing a simple dinner. My grandfather was watching the news, my grandmother was nearby, my mother tried to feed me with gentle insistence. Suddenly, my father arrived. He stood at the iron grill door, shouting profanities. The night air thickened with tension.

As my grandfather tried to keep him outside, my father, drunk and desperate, tapped an alcohol bottle against the metal bars. Perhaps it was mere frustration, perhaps a subconscious desire to break something. The bottle shattered, scattering glass shards inward. A few pieces embedded themselves into my grandfather's stomach. Neighbors rushed over, jolted from their evening routines by the commotion. Some of them beat my father, as though returning a fraction of the violence he had so often unleashed inside our old home. My mother, forced into an impossible role, called the police. Imagine being a child and seeing your father not as a protector but as a chaotic intruder who harms even those who care for you. The police came, took him away, and he spent two days in jail. This moment, in its brutal clarity, confirmed what I had begun to suspect: fathers do not always protect, mothers do not always smile, and the world is not neatly divided into heroes and villains.

Psychologically, such incidents plant seeds that blossom into a garden of distrust. Children depend on caregivers to model stable, kind behavior. When that fails, when love and protection turn into chaos and harm, children learn to question the very foundations of relationship and security. Over time, these experiences can result in anxiety disorders, attachment issues, or an inability to form healthy bonds later in life. I had no language for these concepts then, but my body and mind absorbed the lessons: The world is unsafe. The people you love can hurt you. Crying solves nothing. Trust is fragile.

Not long after this incident, my father decided to return to his village, a place about 45 kilometers away. It was the final time I saw him alive. My mother stayed behind, determined to raise me without the constant shadow of violence. Yet life did not become easy. In fact, it remained a careful balancing act between survival and despair. My mother resumed her work—carrying cylinders, scrubbing floors, washing clothes. My grandfather continued his labor at the plant, coming home covered in dust and sweat, contributing his modest earnings so we could eat. My grandmother managed what little we had, cooking simple meals with quiet efficiency.

I continued to attend school, but education for me had become an uneven battleground. Teachers could be harsh, discipline was often delivered through sticks or slaps, and I was too timid to speak out, too frightened to explain my turmoil. At home, we never discussed these matters. Emotional trauma hovered unspoken in the silence between us. I learned to keep my thoughts and fears inside, a common adaptive strategy for children in unstable environments. Psychologists often note that children lacking a safe space to articulate their feelings grow inward, sometimes becoming anxious, withdrawn, or prone to problem behaviors outside the home. I experimented with truancy, wandering the streets, escaping from one fear only to encounter another. My mother tried to correct me through scoldings and beatings. Discipline without understanding often deepens the cycle of confusion.

Then came the morning that changed everything: January 27, 2007. We received a phone call that my father was dead. In death, he returned suddenly to the center of our story, reshaping all the messy threads of love and hate, violence and silence, into an even more tangled knot. My mother screamed and wept, clutching me so tightly I could hardly breathe. She cursed fate, cursed God, cursed the circumstances that had led to this. She had wanted freedom from his brutality, not the finality of his death. She cried out in agony, as if her heart had been torn from her chest. I stood there, confused. Was I supposed to cry? To feel relief, sorrow, anger? My father's presence in my life had been a source of fear and anguish. Now that he was gone, what was I to feel?

We journeyed to his village, traveling the short but emotionally infinite distance to where his body lay. The house where he rested seemed charged with a strange, heavy energy. People gathered, singing ritual songs, preparing for cremation, grieving in their own ways. I saw him lying on the ground, leaves and rice placed in his mouth, a tradition I only dimly understood. My mother's screams reached a new pitch as she saw him like this—still, lifeless, removed from the world of conflict and torment. I watched the scene with a peculiar detachment, more stunned than tearful. Children sometimes respond to trauma with numbness, a protective mechanism. Maybe my mind was shielding me from the raw enormity of death.

At some point, I hugged my mother, and tears flowed. Fear erupted in me—a fear of what came next, fear of the unknown. Without my father, who were we as a family? Would life be kinder or harsher now that his violence had reached its endpoint? His death, like his life, would ripple through our existence, shaping how my mother and I understood the world and ourselves. According to some studies in bereavement psychology, the death of a parent during childhood can profoundly alter a child's mental development, influencing everything from self-esteem to future relationships. The child is forced to confront mortality and the fragility of life too soon, absorbing complexities that even adults struggle to comprehend.

As the rituals continued, an argument broke out. My father's brother hurled accusations at my mother, blaming her for this death. He used language I would later identify as misogynistic and cruel, calling her names meant to wound and degrade. She responded with fury, defending herself and hurling back accusations, suggesting that they had contributed to his demise. In that charged exchange, I saw not just two grieving people but the collision of worlds: one of patriarchal expectations, blame, and denial, and another of a woman pushed beyond her limits, refusing to be cast as a scapegoat.

For a moment, I understood that this scene wasn't just about my family. It was about how societies handle grief, how they assign blame in the wake of tragedy, how old resentments surface at the worst possible times. It reflected patterns that anthropologists and sociologists often discuss: death as a communal event that can either bring people together or fracture them into opposing camps. In our case, it fractured. My mother's anger, though sharpened by pain, was also a kind of liberation. She refused to be silenced, even now, when sorrow weighed heavily on all hearts. She hinted at the possibility of legal repercussions if her in-laws persisted in their slander. Nothing came of these threats, but they demonstrated her inner steel.

We learned the probable cause of my father's death: a sudden chest pain, possibly a heart attack, while he worked to prepare land for building a house. There was a rumor of a wrong injection given by a local medical attendant. There was talk of rushing him to a distant hospital, of him dying en route. The details remained murky, contested, half-whispered. The truth seemed to dissolve in a haze of regret and speculation. No one wanted to admit their part in it. Was it the alcohol, the stress, the poor medical care, or sheer fate? Children often crave clarity and reason, yet I found none. In that ambiguity, I sensed a lesson: sometimes events are too complex, too layered with human error and misfortune, to yield a neat explanation.

After the cremation and the final mourning rituals, we returned to Sriharipuram. Life had changed again. My mother redoubled her efforts to keep us afloat. She earned around 1500 to 2000 rupees a month as a maid, and my grandparents provided food and shelter. I continued attending school, but the meaning of education was still lost on me. I carried inside me a heavy mix of confusion and shame, a turbulent cocktail of experiences—domestic violence, displacement, a father now gone forever, and a mother struggling to breathe in a world stacked against her.

From a psychological standpoint, these years might be considered a crucial phase of identity formation. The German developmental psychologist Erik Erikson spoke of stages like "industry vs. inferiority" and "identity vs. role confusion," where children and adolescents grapple with their place in the world. My place felt uncertain. Violence had shaped my early worldview. Fear had taught me to run from problems, not confront them. My father's death introduced a profound sense of impermanence. Nothing was stable, nothing guaranteed.

Without guidance, children often drift toward dysfunctional coping mechanisms: avoidance, aggression, or secretive behaviors that temporarily ease the pain but solve nothing.

It is not surprising, then, that around these years I often wandered aimlessly, avoiding classrooms, drifting into activities that offered momentary distraction. If I had known more about how trauma affects concentration and executive function, how constant fear and instability can hamper a child's ability to focus and learn, I might have shown myself more compassion in hindsight. Instead, at the time, I simply felt inadequate, scared of teachers, scared of being beaten, unsure why I was unable to follow the straight path of a normal student. Normality itself felt like a foreign country whose language I did not speak.

My mother's grief and strength coexisted in a delicate balance. She never spoke openly about the pain locked in her memories, at least not to me. Perhaps she lacked the words, or believed that talking to a child would do no good. Perhaps she feared breaking down, worried that if she showed vulnerability, the fragile structure of our new life might collapse. This silence is common in families touched by violence and trauma. Adults often avoid discussing painful topics, hoping children will forget, heal, or never fully understand. But children do not simply forget. The body and mind remember. The nervous system encodes the tension, the fear, the distrust, and these patterns persist until confronted and worked through.

Though I didn't know it at the time, this family silence was part of a broader pattern. Many cultures treat emotional pain and trauma as private matters, to be concealed from outsiders. Others believe children cannot understand complexity, so they shield them. The unintended consequence is that children grow up lacking tools to process their emotions. They feel alone with their fears and confusions. They think something is wrong with them, rather than with the circumstances that shaped them.

As the weeks after my father's death turned into months, I began to sense that life was forging a new equilibrium. It was far from ideal, but it was less chaotic than before. Without my father's unpredictable appearances, our home was quieter. The absence of immediate violence granted a space for small comforts: playing with friends, helping my grandmother with small chores, watching my grandfather return home covered in dust after a day's labor and yet smiling at me with quiet affection.

There were still moments of tension—my mother's frustrations sometimes spilled over into angry scoldings toward me. Lacking another outlet for her pent-up sorrow, she occasionally lashed out. A child might interpret this as a personal failing, but now, looking back, I see it as a tragic cycle: the abused mother, who can never confront the true source of her suffering (since he is gone), displaces her anger onto the nearest available target. It is a common dynamic in trauma-laden households. Emotional energy must go somewhere. Without proper channels—therapy, supportive friends, caring mentors—it is often redirected into the weakest link, the child who cannot fight back.

In these complexities, I find echoes of countless other stories. Some children live through civil wars, others through poverty or pandemics. Many endure the quiet despair of broken homes. Psychologically, these experiences shape how we interpret the world, how we trust or mistrust others, how we conceive of ourselves. While my story is unique in its details—my father's alcohol-fueled rage, his sudden death, my mother's ceaseless labor—the underlying patterns are not. They are woven into the tapestry of human experience. The human mind, molded by early impressions, carries the weight of its formative years long after childhood ends.

At this stage in life, I still had no grand understanding of why I felt the way I did. I did not know the names of the psychological conditions I flirted with, nor the frameworks that might have explained my reactions. All I had were lingering emotions, unspoken questions, and habits that I could not break. I had sadness that could not be expressed in words, anxiety that showed itself in trembling hands and a racing heart, anger that burned quietly beneath the surface.

Perhaps the greatest gift these memories now offer is perspective. They illuminate how fear, loss, and confusion can shape a child's developing psyche. They show how family tragedies create ripples that extend beyond the initial event. My father's death, in all its ambiguity, forced a reckoning: I had to live without him, understand him in absence rather than presence, and grapple with the complicated legacy he left behind.

In the quiet nights that followed his passing, I sometimes lay awake, staring at the shadows cast on the walls by a distant streetlight. My mother, exhausted, slept fitfully in another corner of the house. My grandparents breathed softly in their room. Outside, the world carried on—neighbors whispered, dogs barked, the city groaned under its daily burdens. In that darkness, my mind was a silent observer, cataloging events without fully understanding them.

I had learned that the adults I depended upon were fallible, that the world did not guarantee justice or fairness. Yet I also learned that we survive. Even when understanding is scarce, even when comfort is minimal, we endure day by day. Survival itself is a testament to human adaptability. Perhaps that, more than any philosophical insight, was the raw lesson of my childhood: that we persist, that we hold on to whatever threads we can find, until we can make sense of it all.

II

Seeking Understanding Amid Complexity

3

A World Without Anchors

I recall a morning that broke with a pale, hesitant light, as if the sun itself wasn't sure it wanted to rise. The lanes outside were quiet except for the distant hum of traffic and the occasional bark of a street dog. In my corner of the world, nothing dramatic was happening at that instant—no raised voices, no sudden knocks at the door—but I sensed that something was wrong inside me. I didn't have the language for it then, but it was as if I had grown hollow at the core. Days passed in a kind of muted blur, and I struggled to find any stable point to hold on to.

My life had become a series of evasions. I evaded direct questions, avoided places where I might be confronted, and steered clear of anyone who seemed too curious about what I did with my time. At school, I found myself studying people's faces more than any lesson, trying to guess what lay behind their eyes. Some teachers carried a sternness that I interpreted as permanent disapproval. Some of my classmates seemed confident, walking with heads high and shoulders back, as though life offered them a clear path forward. I envied their certainty. For me, each decision—be it attending a class, speaking up when something felt unfair, or attempting to befriend someone—seemed laden with invisible traps.

Because I had developed a habit of slipping away from what frightened me, I often found myself wandering aimlessly. Sometimes I drifted into parts of the neighborhood I had never explored before: narrow alleys lined with mismatched homes, small shops selling sweets and tea, tiny workshops where men hammered metal or shaped wood. I looked at these people—shopkeepers chatting easily with customers, workers smiling as they wiped sweat from their foreheads—and marveled at how at home they seemed in their own skins. They had skills, tasks, and roles that gave them identity. I, on the other hand, felt undefined. I was neither a diligent student nor a daring rebel. I had no particular talent, no sense of purpose. I was just a presence, a boy moving through spaces without leaving an imprint.

One day, while wandering, I came upon an old stone bench beneath a large neem tree. The tree's leaves whispered softly, moved by a breeze I couldn't feel. It was mid-afternoon, and this corner was oddly peaceful. I sat down, folded my arms on my knees, and tried to think. I tried to remember the last time I had felt honestly happy or proud of myself. Strangely, no memory presented itself with clarity. There were fragments—images of playing a sport as a younger child, overhearing a kind word spoken about me once—but they felt distant and unreal. At this point, even regret felt dull and repetitive.

I had once heard someone say that children learn who they are from the people around them. If that's true, I wondered what I could learn from the people I observed. There was a man who passed by every few days, carrying stacks of newspapers on an old bicycle. He never spoke to me, and I never asked his name, but I noticed that he sang quietly to himself as he rode along, as if finding pleasure in the simple act of doing his job. Then there was a young girl, perhaps a few years younger than me, who darted through the lanes every morning, neatly dressed, her hair combed, a schoolbag on her back, always on time, always brisk and purposeful. I watched her from a distance and thought: What does she know that I don't? How does she move so confidently?

What set these people apart from me? It seemed they had direction. Whether they were delivering newspapers or attending classes, they had routines and aims that made sense to them. In contrast, my goals were hazy. I woke each day unsure of what it would bring. I still found reasons to avoid certain lessons at school. If I sensed a tense mood in a teacher, if I felt I couldn't answer a question, I would slip out, convincing myself I didn't need whatever they were trying to teach. If I noticed a group of students whispering and snickering, I would avoid them too, unwilling to risk their judgment.

In that environment, knowledge about life didn't come from careful guidance; it came from snatched glimpses of other people's behaviors. I learned that if I kept quiet enough, people left me alone. If I nodded without speaking, most would assume I understood or agreed with them. This allowed me to pass unnoticed through many situations, a ghost among the living. But what good was invisibility? It protected me from scoldings, yes, but it also denied me any warmth or connection. I understood fear and avoidance, but not friendship or trust.

Sometimes, I considered changing my approach. I imagined myself walking up to someone—a classmate known for kindness or a neighbor with a friendly smile—and introducing myself properly, asking simple questions, maybe hinting at my confusion. Yet I never mustered the courage. The words tangled on my tongue, and a persistent thought held me back: What if they don't care? What if they laugh at me or dismiss me? Rejection loomed large in my mind, a monster more frightening than isolation.

Without meaningful relationships, my moral compass wavered. I knew certain things were wrong, but that knowledge felt abstract. Why was something wrong? Was it because it harmed others, or because adults said so, or because it made me feel uneasy afterward? I had no framework for understanding morality beyond raw emotion and vague memories of being told what not to do. Values like empathy, respect, or honesty floated around as words I'd heard but never fully embraced. It was easy to make excuses for small misbehaviors when no one took the time to explain their consequences in a way that made sense to me.

During one of my solitary excursions, I passed a small open-air temple. I rarely paid attention to religious spots, but on that day, something made me slow down. Incense curled into the air. A few people stood quietly, heads bowed. An old priest sat near the entrance, his eyes half-closed, humming softly. I watched them from a distance, curious but hesitant. These people seemed to find comfort in devotion. They had a sense of belonging to something larger than themselves. I lingered there for a few minutes, wondering if faith could give people direction. Yet I felt no calling. It was as if my mind was too restless, too anxious to settle into any kind of belief or ritual. I had learned to survive by remaining detached, and detachment does not yield easily to faith or confidence.

As the weeks wore on, I noticed changes in how I felt about mundane things. Tasks that should have been simple—listening to a lesson at school, talking to a classmate about homework—felt complicated. I worried that I would say something stupid or reveal my ignorance. It was easier to remain quiet, nod, and pretend. This habit of pretending became second nature. Pretending not to mind when someone mocked me. Pretending I understood a topic I'd never studied. Pretending I wasn't bothered by my lack of direction. This pretense layered over every interaction, creating a sense of inauthenticity that gnawed at my insides.

I also became more aware of subtle hierarchies around me. Certain boys at school commanded respect because they were good at sports, or because their families were well-regarded. Others gained status through humor or intelligence. I had none of these currencies. I was not particularly athletic, not known for clever jokes, not praised for my marks. If anyone noticed me at all, it was as that boy who drifted in and out of class, who never raised his hand to answer. Some regarded me with mild pity, others with contempt. Most ignored me. Being ignored can feel like safety, but it can also feel like being erased.

Despite all this, I did not completely stop hoping. Sometimes, in rare moments, I imagined a different future. Perhaps one day I would find a mentor—an older student, a kind teacher, or a neighbor—who would take the time to ask me about my thoughts and genuinely listen. Maybe they would share stories of their own struggles, admitting that they, too, had once felt lost. Imagining this gave me a quiet ache, a longing that I tried to bury. Hope can be painful when you have no reason to believe it will be fulfilled.

In my wanderings, I sometimes observed how people resolved their conflicts. I saw shopkeepers argue over deliveries, then reach compromises after heated exchanges. I watched neighbors disagree about trivial matters like where to park a bicycle, eventually settling things with a shrug. Conflicts resolved by communication fascinated me because I rarely witnessed that skill in my own interactions. Here were grown-ups, sometimes raising their voices but then cooling down, listening, and finding solutions. If only I had learned that skill: to voice my doubts calmly, to negotiate my fears with someone willing to understand them.

There were also moments of communal laughter I overheard—groups of friends teasing each other in good-natured ways, chuckling over small jokes. How free and joyful they seemed! Laughter like that never felt forced. It was a relief valve for the pressures of daily life. I realized I lacked that outlet. Without trust, I could not risk laughing openly, could not risk making a joke that fell flat. Everything about me was guarded, calculated for minimal exposure. Living this way was exhausting, though I didn't fully recognize the fatigue at the time.

At certain points, I tried to find small distractions to fill my hours. I might stand near a local cricket ground, not joining the game but watching from the sidelines. I tried to understand the rules better, to see what made the players coordinate effortlessly as a team. They shouted signals, called each other by nicknames, celebrated boundaries, and lamented wickets—but always together. Their cohesion highlighted my isolation. It wasn't about winning or losing; it was about belonging to a group with a shared goal. I had never felt that unity.

Sometimes I studied the walls and doors around the neighborhood, noticing posters or slogans painted in bright colors. Occasional announcements for cultural events—music performances, festivals, or debates—made me wonder what it would be like to attend such gatherings. Could I just blend into the audience and learn something new? But the idea of stepping into an unfamiliar crowd intimidated me. Fear of judgment loomed large. I convinced myself I wouldn't understand what was being discussed, or that people would immediately sense I was out of place.

This anxiety shaped my moral decisions as well. When tempted to do something questionable, I rationalized it by thinking, "Who cares anyway?" or "I have no one to guide me." I felt that without someone showing a better path, I was doomed to repeat mistakes. Yet I also knew that wasn't entirely true—I still had a sense of right and wrong, even if blurred. The problem was, doing the right thing often felt meaningless in a world where I saw no reward for goodness and no immediate punishment for wrongdoings beyond mild guilt. Without clear reasons or role models, moral principles became slippery concepts, easy to dismiss when inconvenient.

But conscience is a stubborn thing. At night, lying in whatever quiet space I could find, I would stare at shadows on the ceiling, shapes formed by faint streetlights filtering through the window. I tried to recall each choice of the day. Did I cheat someone out of something?

Did I ignore a cry for help, even a small one—a classmate struggling with a lesson, a younger child who needed directions? Often, I had not committed any glaring misdeeds, but I had also not done anything kind or constructive. My existence felt neutral at best, purposeless at worst. And that thought troubled me. Life, even at my young age, I suspected, should mean something more than drifting.

Once, I came close to seeking advice from an adult who seemed approachable—a person who worked in a small stationery shop near the school. He looked patient, always arranging pencils and notebooks carefully, smiling gently at customers. For a few afternoons, I hovered near that shop, pretending to examine items, mustering the courage to start a conversation. I imagined asking a simple question: "How do you decide what's right or wrong?" or "Is it normal to feel unsure about everything?" But I never asked. Each time, my voice failed me. My fears of appearing foolish or overly dramatic held me back. Eventually, I stopped visiting that shop, ashamed of my own cowardice.

Another time, I noticed a group of older boys helping a neighbor fix a broken gate. They volunteered their time, lifting heavy boards and hammering nails without complaint. It struck me how natural it seemed for them. They chatted and laughed as they worked, making a dull chore into a communal activity. I wondered if I could do something similar—maybe offer help to someone in need. Would that make me feel more anchored, more worthwhile? Yet I hesitated. Altruism felt risky. What if someone asked why I was helping? What if they suspected I had ulterior motives? My paranoia kept me from testing even that harmless avenue of growth.

The passing of time did not improve my situation. The school year advanced, others grew more comfortable in their identities, and I remained stuck. Some peers made new friends, joined clubs, excelled at subjects, or found hobbies. I stood at the periphery, watching them evolve. Even the younger students looked at me with curiosity, as if trying to categorize me: Was I older or younger, shy or rude, clever or slow? They couldn't place me, and that mirrored my own inability to define myself.

Surprisingly, the absence of overt turmoil was unsettling. Sometimes a crisis forces one to make decisions, to seek help or confront fears. But a mild, ongoing uncertainty allows one to drift indefinitely. There was no emergency to prompt me to change, no large event pushing me to reconsider my direction. This quiet limbo could last forever, I feared, and that thought terrified me more than any punishment. A life of quiet disconnection—was that my fate?

I knew that narratives in books or movies often showed a mentor figure stepping in at critical moments. A teacher notices a struggling student and offers guidance. A neighbor recognizes a lost soul and shares wisdom. But in reality, people are often absorbed in their own problems, blind to subtle signals from someone like me. If help existed, it was not going to materialize out of thin air. That realization pressed on me, demanding that if I ever wanted to change, I would have to find a way myself.

Yet, where to begin? I had no map. Without repeating past lessons or guidance, I had to guess what mattered. Perhaps honesty mattered—being honest with myself about my fears and insecurities. Perhaps curiosity mattered—daring to learn something new, even if it meant risking embarrassment. Perhaps kindness mattered—doing a small good deed without expecting anything in return. These thoughts tiptoed through my mind, but they never settled. I lacked the courage to act on them.

There were days when I tried to observe my own thoughts as if from a distance. Why did I assume everyone would mock me if I spoke up? Why did I believe understanding morality required someone else's explanation? Maybe I had the capacity to reason it out. If harming someone felt wrong because it caused pain, could I not deduce that helping someone might feel right because it relieved suffering? This simple logic was available to me all along, but I had never leaned into it. I was too caught up in fear and uncertainty.

At one point, I toyed with the idea of changing my routine. If my current patterns led to emptiness, what if I did something different each day? Maybe I could start by staying in class an extra ten minutes before running off, gradually building tolerance for discomfort. Or I could nod less and ask at least one genuine question per day. Or I could pick a corner of the neighborhood and imagine what it would be like to approach someone, compliment their work, or ask how their day was going. Small steps, yes, but potentially transformative if followed through.

None of these plans took immediate shape, though. They floated like distant possibilities, comforting in theory but frightening in practice. I recognized a paradox: I yearned for connection and meaning, yet I resisted the vulnerability needed to achieve them. I wanted direction, but refused to take a step into unfamiliar territory. Inertia had claimed me, holding me captive in a state of passive longing.

As the season shifted—days becoming warmer, nights lingering with a different resonance—I realized time was slipping by. My peers grew taller, their voices changing, their interests evolving. They moved forward with the current of adolescence. I remained adrift, an observer at the river's edge. Occasionally, this made me resentful: Why did others seem to have it easier? But I knew I was not seeing their struggles. They might be facing challenges of their own, hidden beneath confident exteriors.

From time to time, I caught myself wishing for someone to recognize my turmoil without me asking. Maybe a stranger would look at me and just know I needed guidance. It was a child's fantasy. Adults, preoccupied with their roles and routines, were not scanning the crowd for lost souls. They expected youths to find their own way or follow the established paths. The world didn't pause for me; I had to catch up or be left behind.

Gradually, I began acknowledging a painful truth: my drift was self-perpetuated. While my circumstances certainly influenced me, at this point I contributed to the cycle by refusing opportunities for growth. Even a kind word to someone else, or a small risk like asking a question in class, could have led to new outcomes. Realizing this stung because it challenged my view of myself as a victim of circumstance. I was not only a product of my environment; I was also an agent, however hesitant, in shaping my experience.

This insight did not immediately liberate me. Fear still outweighed hope. Yet, the seed of understanding was planted. I now knew I had some power, however limited, to change. To exercise it would require mustering courage I hadn't shown before. It would mean choosing discomfort over numbness, sincerity over pretense, and action over silence. These were not easy choices.

As the chapter of my life continued, I remained mostly stuck, but not entirely unaware. I felt a subtle tension inside—a tension between the old, fearful self I inhabited and a potential self who might one day learn to speak, to act, to care, and to connect. That possibility was faint, but it was there, a quiet whisper reminding me that I was alive and capable of growth.

In the moments before sleep, listening to distant voices drifting through the night air, I tried to imagine a scenario where I took a small step forward. Perhaps I would greet someone I usually avoided. Perhaps I would stay in class and attempt to solve a simple problem on the board. Perhaps I would admit to myself that I was lost, and that recognizing that fact was the first step toward finding a path. These were only visions in the darkness, but they proved I still had an imagination, a capacity to dream.

No one around me noticed these silent battles. They saw a boy who kept to himself, who didn't cause trouble but didn't excel either. They saw no fierce rebellion, no dramatic breakdown, no extraordinary effort. Yet, inside, a profound conflict raged. I was struggling to define who I was and who I wanted to become. Without repeating old explanations or old justifications, I was forced to look inward for answers. The emptiness inside me was both a curse and a blank slate. If I dared, I could fill it with meaning.

Change did not happen overnight, and as this chapter ends, I must admit I had not yet escaped the undertow of uncertainty. But I had begun to question it. Questioning, as I would later learn, is often the first step out of any trap.

4

Small Steps Toward the Light

Late one afternoon, I stood on a cracked patch of pavement, watching the dust settle in the warm light. The world around me had its patterns—schooldays that drained into aimless wanderings, evenings that crept along with the same dull throb of uncertainty. Yet I sensed something stirring inside me, a gentle pressure behind my ribs, as if my heart were nudging me forward. I could no longer deny that I wanted to change my circumstances. Drifting had brought me no comfort; avoiding people and challenges had only deepened my loneliness. For the first time, I felt a quiet determination to alter my approach, even if it meant taking uncertain steps into unfamiliar territory.

I did not expect miracles. There was no grand revelation, no sudden hero arriving to guide me. Instead, there was a subtle decision forming in my mind: I would try small experiments, gentle attempts to connect or learn something new. I would not declare these intentions aloud, for fear that speaking them might shatter my fragile resolve. But inside, I whispered to myself: "Try something different. Just one small thing."

My first experiment began with a moment of observation. Near the place where I often wandered—those narrow lanes where I watched people at their trades—I noticed a young man who tended a tiny roadside library stand. It wasn't a proper library, merely a makeshift wooden shelf set outside a shopfront, holding a jumble of worn paperbacks and cheap magazines. Most people passed by without a glance. But I was curious. I had never spent much time reading. Words intimidated me, especially since my grasp of language felt shaky. Still, the sight of that shelf offered a possibility: here was something I could explore quietly, without demanding anyone's attention. Perhaps I could learn a new pattern, discover new ideas, or simply find a moment of peace.

One evening, as shadows stretched across the street, I approached the shelf. The man who managed it stood nearby, chatting with someone else. He had a gentle manner—no fixed smile, but no scowl either. He looked like the kind of person who found contentment in small routines. Without interrupting his conversation, I scanned the titles. Most were too advanced for me or looked uninteresting at first glance. Stories of distant lands, philosophical essays I wouldn't understand, old textbooks with yellowing pages. But then my eyes settled on a slim volume that bore a simple cover: a plain background with a small illustration of a tree and a bird. The title was something about understanding oneself. That idea intrigued me. Understanding oneself—was that possible from printed words?

I hesitated, uncertain if I could simply pick a book and look through it. The man finished talking with his acquaintance and turned to me. I met his gaze for a second and quickly looked away. He did not speak, nor did he shoo me off. Emboldened by his silence, I lifted the book gently, as if it might crumble in my hands. He nodded slightly, giving permission without words.

I stepped back and found a quiet corner to sit on a low wall. The noise of traffic was distant enough not to distract me. I opened the book and tried to read. The language was simpler than I feared, though still requiring effort. The first pages discussed how many people drift through life without asking themselves what they truly feel or think. I almost laughed at the coincidence—this writer described a pattern of uncertainty and confusion that sounded like my own reflection in a mirror. The sentences invited the reader to look inward, to pay attention to fears and desires, to notice how certain habits arise.

Though I did not fully grasp every idea, something resonated. It felt as though a stranger, across time and space, understood that human beings can feel lost, and that this feeling is not unique. This realization didn't solve my problems, but it soothed me. I read slowly, pausing often, letting each paragraph sink in. The writing suggested that people can learn to direct their energies with small acts of courage—asking a question when afraid to, offering help when unsure if it's needed, admitting confusion rather than pretending understanding.

When I finally closed the book and placed it back on the shelf, I did so with careful hands. The young man glanced at me again, not demanding any explanation. I offered the smallest nod of thanks, then drifted away. A seed of thought took root in my mind: perhaps I was allowed to explore knowledge at my own pace. Perhaps reading could help me find words for what I had been feeling. I resolved to return on another day and try something else from that shelf. It was a minor victory, but a victory nonetheless.

A few days later, I made another attempt at engagement, this time involving another human being. I had noticed, on several occasions, a younger boy outside a tiny grocery stall. He often stood there holding a basket of fresh produce, offering customers help packing their vegetables or carrying goods a short distance for a few coins. He couldn't have been more than ten or eleven, smaller than me. Yet I admired how he approached each day with a steady determination, calling out friendly greetings to anyone who passed. There was a quiet dignity in his work, though humble, and he handled rejection—when people brushed him off—without bitterness.

One afternoon, I dared to linger near him. He noticed me lingering and offered a polite greeting: "Hello, did you need something?" I had not prepared a script. Panic flared. Should I ask a question? Make some excuse? For a moment, my throat tightened, and I nearly walked away. But I remembered the words I had read, the notion of admitting confusion rather than pretending understanding. I took a breath and said quietly, "I'm just looking around." It was hardly profound, but it was honest. The boy shrugged amicably and continued calling out to potential customers, as if my presence mattered neither negatively nor positively. I was free to remain or leave without judgment.

I chose to remain a bit longer, watching how he interacted. When a woman approached and asked about prices, he responded cheerfully. When another person scoffed and walked off, he didn't frown or curse. He just continued his task. Eventually, I asked, "Do you ever get tired of standing here?" He turned to me, surprised I'd spoken more than a single sentence. "Sometimes," he answered, "but I like helping. Some people are kind, and that makes it feel worthwhile."

Kindness. The word struck me. I had not thought much about kindness as a tangible thing. I had seen people help each other occasionally, but I rarely considered what motivated them. Here was a boy younger than me who accepted the uncertainty of how others would treat him, yet he still chose to help. That was a lesson, subtle but significant. Perhaps kindness didn't need grand gestures; it could live in small, everyday acts. I thanked him quietly and left, not wanting to overstay my welcome and risk awkwardness. As I walked away, I felt a sense of warmth. I had spoken to someone and learned something without catastrophe. Another small step.

Encouraged by these experiments, I decided to try something more challenging. I would choose a situation at school that normally frightened me and attempt a different response. Usually, when a teacher asked a question and no one answered immediately, an uncomfortable silence filled the room. In those silences, I shrank, praying not to be chosen. But what if, just once, I tried to answer—even if I was unsure? The idea made my heart pound, but I reasoned that nothing truly catastrophic would happen. At worst, I might get corrected or scolded. At best, I might discover I could survive discomfort and learn from it.

The next morning, I prepared myself mentally. In a mathematics lesson, the teacher posed a problem on the board. She asked if anyone knew how to find the solution. My instincts screamed for me to look down, remain invisible. But I remembered my promise to try. Slowly, I raised my hand, not high and proud but just enough that it could be noticed. The teacher's eyes flickered my way with mild surprise. She nodded, and I stood, my voice trembling slightly as I tried to explain my reasoning. I got halfway through before stumbling over a detail I didn't fully understand. My explanation faltered. Another student snickered softly.

I expected immediate humiliation. But the teacher did not shout. She walked to the board and, using my attempt as a starting point, gently corrected my approach. She said, "You're close. Consider this step differently," and rewrote part of the problem. I listened, heart still pounding, yet I managed to follow her logic. When I sat down, I felt strangely relieved. I had not answered perfectly, but I had shown effort. The teacher's calm response astonished me. Instead of dismissing my attempt, she guided me. Though I still felt a flicker of embarrassment, I also felt a spark of pride. I had broken my pattern of silence and survived.

That night, I reflected on these small risks I had taken. They did not transform me into a confident person overnight, nor did they erase my doubts. But they showed me that change was possible through incremental steps. Each time I tried something new—borrowing a book, speaking to the younger boy, attempting a school problem—I learned that the world did not collapse on me. Instead, my world grew slightly wider. I began to suspect that growth was a slow, uneven process, and that patience mattered as much as courage.

As days passed, I became more attentive to the subtle interactions occurring around me. I noticed how people negotiated their differences through words. I saw that apologies were sometimes offered and accepted. I observed that not every person who scolded or criticized was cruel; sometimes they were simply stressed or trying to maintain order. This recognition allowed me to reinterpret my past fears. Maybe not everyone was waiting to mock me. Maybe many people were just navigating their own difficulties, and my silence had prevented me from seeing the complexity of their intentions.

I also realized how vital self-awareness could be. Reading a few more pages from that roadside library's books, I discovered repeated themes: individuals who learn to observe their own fears and desires can shape their behavior more thoughtfully. This inspired me to analyze my own habits. Why did I feel anxious in certain situations? Often, it was because I expected rejection or ridicule. But now that I had risked minor embarrassment and found it survivable, could I not push a bit further next time?

One afternoon, I decided to perform a small act of kindness, inspired by that younger boy's example. I noticed a classmate struggling to carry a stack of notebooks from the classroom to a storage room. Normally, I would pretend not to see, fearing that offering help might lead to an awkward exchange or expose me to unnecessary scrutiny. But this time, I approached and said, "Do you need a hand?" My classmate glanced at me, surprised, and then nodded gratefully. We carried the notebooks together in silence. When we finished, she said a simple "Thanks," and I responded with a quiet "You're welcome." Nothing dramatic occurred, but I felt a spark of satisfaction. I had contributed something small and harmless without complication. It made me wonder: how many opportunities to connect or assist had I missed simply because I assumed they would be painful?

These small experiments began to accumulate in my mind, forming a mosaic of new experiences. Nothing had radically changed—I was still cautious, still uncertain—but I saw glimmers of another way of being. Perhaps I could learn to trust, at least a little. Perhaps I could seek information when confused, ask questions when lost, and occasionally give without expecting anything in return. This emergent understanding felt fragile, as if a sudden setback could send me back into my shell. Yet each positive experience strengthened my resolve.

At times, I still struggled. On certain days, I woke up feeling weary and doubtful, questioning whether these small steps meant anything in the grand scheme of my life. Was I truly making progress, or just playing at pretend courage? On those days, I forced myself to remember that progress need not be linear or immediately visible. I told myself that even if I felt no different, my behaviors had changed, and behavior often leads understanding. As I acted more openly, maybe I would come to feel more natural about it.

The concept of moral choices began to fascinate me. I had previously considered morality as a set of rules enforced by authority figures. Now I started to see it as a personal compass that could guide me toward healthier relationships and greater understanding. Being honest, helpful, or brave wasn't about obeying some external command; it was about cultivating a better life for myself and others. I realized that morality could be self-motivated, growing from empathy and reflection rather than fear of punishment.

I also learned that empathy requires imagination. To empathize, I had to imagine what another person might be feeling. Observing the younger boy at the grocery stall, I considered his perspective—how he balanced his pride with the need to accept rejections, how he found meaning in small gestures of support from strangers. Thinking this way made me appreciate his resilience. Observing my classmates, I tried to guess what struggles they might face at home or in their minds. This didn't mean I became friends with everyone, but it reduced my tendency to see them as threats. They were human beings with their own lives and burdens.

On another afternoon, I decided to take a more intellectual risk. I returned to the roadside library stand and picked another book, this time something slightly more challenging—a collection of short pieces discussing how people form communities and support each other. The text mentioned cultural traditions, social norms, and how different societies foster cooperation. Some parts were difficult for me, but I gleaned insights: that trust and understanding do not arise in isolation; they are built over time as people learn to communicate and negotiate differences. This knowledge comforted me. If humans learned to cooperate across language barriers, religious differences, and national borders, surely I could learn to cooperate with a few classmates or neighbors.

One evening, reflecting on these readings, I realized I had rarely considered the broader world. I had been so focused on my immediate environment—my own fears, the local streets, the school corridors—that I forgot people everywhere grapple with uncertainty. The book hinted that countless others throughout history had faced confusion, moral dilemmas, and a lack of direction. They had overcome these challenges by building relationships, sharing stories, and passing down lessons. This gave me a sense of continuity. I was not the first person to feel lost, nor would I be the last.

As I absorbed these lessons, I tried a new approach at school: when I didn't understand a concept, instead of quietly panicking or feigning comprehension, I ventured to ask the teacher after class. The first time I did this, my voice trembled slightly, but the teacher responded patiently, showing me a detail I had overlooked. She seemed pleased that I bothered to inquire. Another small step: I could now seek help rather than hiding my ignorance.

I tried something similar with a classmate who was good at a subject that baffled me. Initially, I was afraid they would mock me for not knowing something so "obvious." But when I asked for clarification, they explained it without hesitation. In that moment, I learned that many people enjoy sharing what they know, feeling valued when their knowledge helps someone else. My fear had been a barrier, but not a permanent one.

Of course, not every attempt ended so positively. Once, I approached a group discussing a topic I found interesting. My interruption was met with cold indifference; they barely acknowledged my presence. I retreated, stung by their rejection. But instead of interpreting this as proof that all efforts were futile, I tried to remember the successes. Not everyone would welcome me kindly, and that was okay. Learning to accept rejection as part of life was another skill I needed to develop. The world was composed of varied individuals, and not all encounters would bear fruit.

Another time, I misunderstood someone's request and ended up offering help where it wasn't needed, which caused mild annoyance. In the past, I would have taken this as a sign to never offer help again. But now, I accepted it as a lesson in reading situations more carefully. Making mistakes was part of growth. Overcoming shame required acknowledging that I, like everyone else, was imperfect. If I could forgive myself for these small errors, I could keep trying.

As my experiments continued, I noticed subtle internal changes. I started feeling slightly less tense around people. I still disliked large groups and still preferred quiet corners, but I no longer felt that every human interaction was a battle. I learned to breathe through discomfort and remind myself that not knowing the outcome of a conversation did not doom me. Curiosity began replacing dread. Instead of asking, "What if this goes wrong?" I tried asking, "What might I learn from this?"

This shift in perspective also influenced how I saw authority figures. I had once viewed teachers and adults as either threats or distant forces beyond my understanding. Now, by engaging with them more openly—asking questions, responding to prompts—I realized they were people doing their jobs, some patient and others less so. Their criticisms were not always personal attacks; sometimes they aimed to push me to do better. Their praise, though rare, felt more genuine when I knew I had earned it by attempting something challenging.

In turning inward to examine my fears, I discovered a pattern: many fears shrank once faced. They did not vanish completely—I still worried about making a fool of myself—but they lost their ability to paralyze me. By surviving small embarrassments, I realized I could endure bigger ones if they ever arose. That provided a sense of resilience I'd never known before.

I also started to understand that identity is not fixed. I had thought of myself as "the quiet, anxious one," defined by hesitations and insecurities. But the more I acted differently, the more I saw that identity can evolve. If I could be the person who raises his hand in class or offers help, even occasionally, then I was not locked into my old image. I could rewrite my story. This realization filled me with cautious hope. Life, it seemed, might be more flexible than I had assumed.

The books I borrowed continued to shape my thinking. One text described how societies rely on shared narratives—common values, myths, and histories that give people a sense of belonging. While I did not yet feel I belonged anywhere special, the idea that humans create meaning together fascinated me. Maybe I had to find or create my own narrative. Maybe I could start by defining small principles for myself: honesty when confused, kindness when possible, curiosity instead of avoidance. These weren't grand moral laws, but personal guidelines that could help me move through the world with more confidence.

Another text mentioned the importance of listening. I realized I had rarely listened deeply to anyone. Fear often filled my mind with internal chatter: "What if they judge me?" or "How do I escape this situation?" As a result, I never fully heard what others were saying. What if I tried to listen more attentively, focusing on their words rather than my own insecurities? This experiment intrigued me. The next time someone spoke to me—my teacher explaining a concept, a classmate commenting on something unrelated to school—I concentrated on their tone, their choice of words, their facial expressions. To my surprise, when I truly listened, I understood them better. And understanding reduced my fear. Knowledge replaced guesswork, making the interaction less threatening.

As these internal shifts accumulated, I began noticing changes in my surroundings. Or perhaps the surroundings stayed the same, and I noticed more because I was more engaged. I heard laughter and realized it wasn't always at someone's expense—often it was shared joy. I saw people disagree but then find common ground. I witnessed small acts of generosity that I would have overlooked before: a student lending a pen to another without fuss, someone picking up a dropped notebook and returning it with a smile. These scenes contrasted sharply with the world I had imagined when I was trapped in fear. The difference lay in where I chose to focus my attention.

It dawned on me that my perspective had once been narrowed by anxiety, filtering out positive examples and amplifying threats. As I practiced new behaviors, I recalibrated this filter. I could see more nuance: kindness coexisted with indifference, patience with impatience, but now I recognized both sides. This balanced view freed me from the despair of assuming everyone and everything was hostile. It also reminded me that I, too, had a responsibility. If I wanted to live in a world with more understanding, I had to contribute to that understanding in my small way.

This mindset did not arise from a single dramatic moment. It was the cumulative result of many small efforts: reading those books, asking a teacher for help, offering assistance to a classmate, enduring rejection without giving up, and daring to speak when I was uncertain. Together, these acts formed a quiet revolution within me. They did not make me fearless or extroverted overnight, but they replaced my old narrative of paralysis with one of cautious growth.

One day, as I passed by the younger boy at the grocery stall again, he recognized me and nodded. This time, I said, "Keep it up," and he grinned, replying, "Thanks!" That tiny exchange was like a handshake with the world, affirming that I was not invisible or condemned to isolation. Another day, the teacher who had corrected my math problem looked at me expectantly during a lesson, and I dared to raise my hand again, this time with slightly more confidence.

These small shifts would have been unimaginable before. If I could tell my past self that I would one day do these things, he would not believe me. That realization inspired me to think about the future. If I kept practicing this gradual approach, what else might become possible? Maybe I would one day find it easier to make friends or contribute to a discussion without panic. Maybe I could discover talents or interests I had never explored because I was too busy hiding.

I also understood that setbacks would continue. Not every interaction would end well, not every question would be well-received. The world remained complicated, people remained unpredictable, and I remained human—capable of errors and misunderstandings. But embracing imperfection was part of maturity. I had learned that growth does not demand perfection; it demands patience, honesty, and the willingness to keep trying despite difficulties.

In quiet moments, I considered the deeper implications of these lessons. Morality, I realized, is woven from how we treat each other in countless small encounters. Philosophy, which once seemed like a distant domain of abstract thinking, now felt relevant to my daily choices. I saw how philosophical ideas—the nature of fear, the value of empathy, the construction of meaning—played out in the subtle gestures of everyday life. This understanding humbled me. It showed me that wisdom is not confined to scholars and sages; it can be found in a child offering help, in a teacher's patient correction, in a stranger allowing me to browse a book without questioning.

My transformation, if I could call it that, was still in its infancy. I had not become a different person entirely, only nudged myself toward a more open and curious approach to living. I had begun to accept that understanding oneself and others is a lifelong endeavor. Just as I had learned to decode a difficult sentence in a book by reading slowly and looking up unfamiliar words, I could learn to decode human interactions and moral dilemmas through practice, reflection, and humility.

As I stood at another crossroads of dusty lanes one late afternoon, feeling the warmth of the sun on my face, I realized that my sense of emptiness was beginning to ebb. In its place, I felt a quiet sense of direction. Not a rigid path laid out before me, but a compass that pointed toward honesty, compassion, and curiosity. I still had a long way to go. I still felt uncertain about many things, still had days when fear whispered that I should retreat into silence. But now I had evidence that pushing against that fear could yield richer experiences.

I understood that I was constructing my identity bit by bit. No one would hand me a blueprint. No one would assure me that I was doing it right. But by acting, observing consequences, and adjusting my approach, I could shape my character. And character, I realized, was what guided you when rules were unclear and fate offered no guarantees. If I cultivated empathy, courage, and understanding, I would be better equipped to face whatever lay ahead.

In this way, I began to see my personal struggles reflected in a wider human narrative. History and literature were filled with people who overcame obstacles not by grand heroic acts, but by steady perseverance, by learning from mistakes, and by reaching out toward others. I was not alone in this process. I stood in a lineage of countless individuals who had felt lost and found their way inch by inch.

The sun dipped lower, casting long shadows. As I walked home, each step felt lighter. I had made no grand announcements to anyone, but my private resolve was firm: I would continue these experiments—speaking up when I was unsure, listening more attentively, extending help where possible, asking when I didn't understand. Over time, these experiments might rewrite my fears into something more manageable. They might grant me the confidence to face life with a measure of grace.

What mattered now was not immediate success or recognition, but consistency. Small steps, repeated over time, could lead me toward the light I had once thought unreachable. And even if the light remained distant, striving toward it felt meaningful. That meaning alone was enough to sustain me. I carried that thought with me as I turned a corner and vanished into the soft twilight, hopeful that tomorrow would bring more opportunities to learn and grow.

III

Finding a Voice and Purpose

5

Shaping a Voice of My Own

A few weeks passed after I began taking those tentative steps toward openness, each day adding a subtle note of confidence to my interactions. The changes were still modest—I hadn't transformed into a fearless speaker or formed deep friendships overnight—but I noticed that my shoulders felt less tense when I entered the classroom, and my eyes lingered less on the floor when a teacher addressed me. I dared to smile, even faintly, at people I recognized in the corridors. Some smiled back, some simply carried on, but the point was that my world no longer seemed so forbidding.

One crisp morning, as I made my way to school, I saw a flyer pasted crookedly on a wall near the roadside library stand. The paper was weathered and slightly torn at the edges, but the words were still visible: "Community Reading Circle—All Are Welcome. Sunday, 5 PM." My heart gave a curious flutter. A reading circle? The thought both intrigued and unsettled me. On one hand, it sounded like an environment where I might be forced to speak before strangers or show ignorance. On the other hand, it promised the chance to learn from people who also cared about words and ideas. I lingered near the poster, reading it again and again, as if searching for a hidden code that would tell me what to do.

By now, I understood that my old patterns of avoidance led nowhere. I remembered how picking up a simple book from that roadside shelf had revealed new perspectives. Perhaps attending the reading circle would extend my understanding even further. And if it turned awkward or overwhelming, I could always leave quietly. The idea of giving myself permission to leave if necessary felt like a safety net, making the whole endeavor seem less daunting.

That Sunday evening, I stood at the appointed place: a small, open courtyard behind a local temple. There were a few benches arranged in a rough circle, with people seated scatteredly. Some looked older, with lines of experience etched on their faces; others were young adults, holding worn books or thin pamphlets. A girl around my age adjusted her glasses and leafed through pages silently. Nobody wore name tags or uniforms—this was not a formal event. It felt more like a spontaneous gathering of those who shared a quiet interest.

I chose a spot at the edge of a bench, willing myself to remain calm. My heart beat faster, but I reminded myself: I had faced discomfort before and survived. As people chatted softly, I listened without speaking. Soon, a middle-aged man stood up, cleared his throat, and introduced himself as Ravi. He explained that the reading circle met every fortnight to share stories, discuss books, and sometimes read aloud short passages. Anyone could participate, and there was no judgment if someone only wanted to listen.

Ravi's kind, open manner put me at ease. One by one, a few individuals shared something. An older woman read a short poem she'd composed about the changing seasons. A college student talked about a biography he found inspiring. A young mother mentioned a children's story that resonated with her.

I watched all this, fascinated. Nobody laughed mockingly or criticized harshly. When someone finished speaking, the others nodded or asked gentle questions. Even disagreements were handled politely, with people taking turns to clarify their points. This cooperative spirit felt like a demonstration of everything I had recently learned in theory but rarely witnessed in practice. Here was a small community forging understanding through words and patience.

Then Ravi asked if anyone new would like to share something or speak about a book they enjoyed. My throat tightened. I had no prepared speech. I owned no special book to discuss. But I did have the memory of that first volume I'd read at the roadside shelf—the one about understanding oneself and facing fears. Even if I didn't remember every word, I recalled how it made me feel less alone. Perhaps mentioning that experience could be my contribution. My stomach churned at the thought of speaking, but I reminded myself I could always keep it brief.

Raising my hand felt like lifting a heavy weight, but I did it. A few people turned their heads my way, curious and not hostile. I cleared my throat, voice shaky at first. "I… I'm new here," I began, words halting. "I don't have a particular book with me, but I once read something from the roadside stand that talked about how people often drift through life without asking questions. It encouraged looking inward and understanding our fears. It helped me realize I'm not alone in feeling uncertain."

I paused, expecting some reaction—maybe confusion or dismissal. Instead, a gentle murmur of approval spread through the group. Ravi nodded. "That's a valuable insight," he said kindly. Another participant commented, "It's true, many of us never stop to reflect, and reading can spark that process." The girl with glasses smiled in my direction, as if to acknowledge my effort.

Relief flooded me. I had spoken in front of strangers and not only survived, but also contributed something meaningful. Even my shaky voice hadn't mattered. What counted was the honesty. For the remainder of the meeting, I listened more than I spoke, but I felt like a participant, not an outsider. After the circle ended, a few people lingered. Ravi caught my eye and said, "I'm glad you spoke up. Keep reading, keep thinking." I mumbled a quiet thank-you before heading home, heart lighter than it had been in a long time.

Over the next days and weeks, this experience stayed with me. I reflected on the reading circle as proof that communities can form around shared curiosity and respect. I had learned that people who value understanding welcome newcomers and their tentative voices. This realization emboldened me further at school. If I could speak among strangers, maybe I could also participate more fully in the classroom or with acquaintances in the neighborhood.

I decided to build on this momentum by pursuing a small personal project: writing down my thoughts. Until now, I had kept everything locked in my mind, never daring to record my feelings for fear they would look foolish on paper. But writing, I reasoned, might help me sort through confusion, just as reading had illuminated others' struggles.

One quiet afternoon, I found a cheap notebook at home—its cover plain blue, its pages lined and slightly yellowed. I opened it and hesitated, pen in hand. What should I write? I wasn't sure. Perhaps I could start by describing my recent experiments, my attempts to speak up, to help, to ask questions. So I wrote a few sentences: "Today, I remembered the time I first picked up a book from the roadside stand. I felt scared, but I learned something new about myself. Fear does not always predict reality."

My handwriting looked uneven, my phrasing clumsy. I worried that someone might find this notebook and mock me. Then I realized: this was for me, not for approval. I continued writing, capturing small moments of growth: helping a classmate, asking a teacher for clarification, speaking at the reading circle. Writing made these memories feel more permanent, something I could revisit when doubts resurfaced.

As I wrote, I noticed patterns. Each positive experience involved stepping out of my comfort zone. Each small success was preceded by hesitation and fear. Yet each time, reality turned out less terrifying than my imagination. This pattern suggested that while fear might never vanish, I could learn to move through it, trusting that even mistakes were survivable. I recorded that insight in my notebook, underlining it as if it were a key lesson.

As my confidence grew, I also became more alert to the needs of others. I started to notice when someone appeared uncomfortable, just as I once had been, and I considered if I could offer them understanding. One morning, I spotted a classmate—someone I scarcely knew—looking anxious before a test. Usually, I would've ignored such tension, assuming it wasn't my place to intervene. But now I thought differently. I remembered how simple words of encouragement, like the ones I'd received, made a difference.

Approaching quietly, I said, "These tests can be stressful. You okay?" She looked up, surprised I had spoken. After a pause, she sighed and admitted she felt unprepared and nervous. I didn't have any grand advice—I was no expert—but I said, "I've felt that way too. Maybe just focus on one question at a time, see what you know. Sometimes worrying makes it worse." She nodded, a weak smile forming. "Thanks. Maybe you're right."

I walked away feeling strangely proud. I hadn't solved her problem, but I offered empathy. This small exchange reaffirmed something crucial: I didn't have to be flawless or all-knowing to support someone else. Simply acknowledging their feelings could help. This understanding aligned with what I'd observed in the reading circle—no one there boasted superior knowledge; they just shared thoughts and listened.

My growing ease in communicating also led me to wonder if I could form a genuine friendship. I had acquaintances in class, people I spoke to occasionally, but I never allowed myself to hope for more. Perhaps it was time to take a bolder step: inviting someone to share an activity outside of the classroom context. The thought made me nervous. What if they refused? Still, I knew rejection wouldn't destroy me. I'd faced worse fears already.

There was a boy named Arun in my class who seemed approachable. He was neither the most popular nor the most withdrawn—just someone who answered questions calmly, smiled politely, and sometimes lent a pen to others without fuss. I decided to test the waters by asking a simple question after a school day: "Hey, Arun, have you ever visited that roadside library stand near the temple?"

He looked at me, brow slightly raised. "I've passed by it, but never stopped," he admitted. "Why?"

I shrugged, trying to sound casual. "I found some interesting books there. They have a reading circle sometimes. Maybe you'd like to check it out with me?"

My heart thumped. Inviting someone felt like stepping off a ledge—would he say yes or find it strange?

"Reading circle?" Arun repeated, intrigued. "That sounds... different. I'm not much of a reader, but it could be interesting."

He didn't say yes immediately, but he didn't mock me either. After thinking for a moment, he nodded. "All right, sure, why not? Let me know when it's happening again."

I let out a breath I hadn't realized I was holding. "Great. I'll let you know." Even if this plan never materialized, the simple fact that he hadn't turned me down flat felt like progress. It showed me that people can be open to new experiences if approached kindly.

As I continued these small social ventures, I also revisited the notebook at home, writing about them. The act of writing helped me notice how each step, no matter how minor, built on the last. If I ever faced a setback—like someone ignoring me or a teacher scolding me harshly—I could flip back through the pages and remind myself of the times when courage led to positive outcomes. This record became my personal guidebook, affirming that I was capable of growth.

Another detail struck me: the moral dimension of my actions. Initially, I had thought morality was about rules—what to do or not to do. But now I saw morality as linked to empathy, understanding, and honesty. By choosing to interact more openly, I recognized the humanity in others. Morality was not a rigid code; it was an evolving practice of treating people with respect and kindness, and striving to understand their perspectives. It felt good to align my actions with these values, especially since they made my world more welcoming.

Encouraged by these reflections, I tried something new at the reading circle on my next visit. Instead of just mentioning a past reading experience, I brought a short poem I had attempted to write. I had never shown anyone my writing—besides my personal notes—and it felt risky. Would they laugh at my simple verses?

When my turn came, I explained that I was experimenting with writing and read the poem aloud. It was short and uncomplicated, about noticing small acts of kindness in daily life. My voice trembled, but I pushed through. When I finished, there was a gentle silence. Then someone said, "That's a lovely sentiment, capturing how ordinary kindness matters." Another added, "I appreciate how you focused on small, real things rather than big, abstract ideas." I smiled, relieved and grateful. This encouragement confirmed that vulnerability, when shared in a supportive setting, could lead to affirmation rather than shame.

Back at school, I found that my willingness to engage with others was subtly altering how some classmates viewed me. Whereas before I might have been invisible or easily overlooked, now a few actually said hello in passing. One asked my opinion on a homework question, and another inquired if I'd seen a certain movie. These were small gestures, but they told me that by stepping forward, I had entered their mental maps as a person worth acknowledging. I realized that I had once feared interaction because I assumed others would judge me negatively, but I never considered that people might have no strong opinion at all until I gave them a reason to care.

My teachers also seemed more receptive to my efforts in class. By occasionally raising my hand or asking questions after a lesson, I showed them I wasn't just idle or disinterested. One teacher even smiled and said, "I'm glad you're taking part, keep it up," as I left class one day. These small validations built upon one another, strengthening my resolve to continue exploring connections and responsibilities.

I also learned to accept that I wouldn't get along with everyone. Some students remained distant or occasionally snide, and not every conversation flowed easily. Sometimes I stumbled over words or offered help where it wasn't wanted. But these missteps no longer felt catastrophic. I had a growing toolkit of coping strategies: I could back away politely, try again another time, or focus on the positive interactions I'd had. Not every situation required me to prove myself or win approval. This realization was freeing; it took pressure off and reminded me that being human meant navigating a range of responses, not all of them favorable.

As I continued to reflect in my notebook, I noticed that my initial motivations had evolved. I had started seeking connection and understanding to overcome fear and find personal comfort. Now, I found that I wanted these things not just for my own sake, but because they contributed to a richer, more compassionate environment. When I listened better, offered encouragement, or dared to share my thoughts, I influenced the atmosphere around me. This influence might be small, barely noticeable, but each act of goodwill counted. It was like adding drops of clear water to a murky pool—the pool might never become perfectly pure, but it would grow clearer over time.

Empowered by these insights, I considered taking on a new challenge: volunteering for a small school event. There was a cultural day approaching, where students were invited to help set up displays or assist teachers with organizing materials. Normally, I would avoid such events, fearing I'd look foolish or get stuck in a task I couldn't handle. But now I thought: this could be another chance to learn something, to meet new people, and to be useful.

Nerves danced in my stomach as I approached the teacher organizing the event. "Excuse me," I said, voice steadier than before, "I'd like to help with the cultural day setup. Is that possible?"

The teacher, who I'd never spoken to much, looked over a clipboard and nodded. "Sure. We could use help arranging chairs and putting up posters. Think you can manage that?"

I swallowed. Arranging chairs and posters? It sounded simple enough. "Yes, I can do that."

On the morning of the event, I arrived early. A few other volunteers were there—students I recognized but didn't know well. We worked side by side, hanging posters carefully, aligning chairs, and making sure everything looked welcoming. While we worked, we exchanged a few casual comments about the decorations or the weather. Nothing profound, but the camaraderie of working together made me feel like I belonged. When we finished, the teacher said, "Great job, everyone! Thank you for your help." My chest swelled with quiet pride. I had contributed, and it had cost me no pain, only a willingness to try.

That evening, I wrote in my notebook: "Today, I helped set up for the cultural day. It might seem small, but it felt meaningful to see something I contributed to taking shape. When people arrive tomorrow, they won't know I helped, but I'll know. And that knowledge is enough to make me feel part of something larger."

My growing confidence didn't mean I had no doubts. Sometimes, I still woke up feeling anxious for no clear reason, worried that one bad interaction would undo my progress. But then I remembered that I had documented so many positive moments, encountered so much understanding, and learned to cope with minor setbacks. My perspective had widened. I now saw that life was not a tightrope stretched over a chasm where one slip spelled doom. It was more like a broad landscape, with many paths to choose from. A stumble on one path didn't prevent me from walking another.

This realization made me curious about the future. What else could I attempt in time? Maybe I could join a small discussion group at school or offer to read something aloud at the reading circle. Maybe I could ask Arun again to visit the reading circle or the roadside library and see how he reacted. Even if these new attempts failed, I knew I'd learn something. Over time, my capacity to handle failure had grown, which paradoxically freed me to try more things without fear of failure crushing me.

I began to see my life's story as something I could shape, not a script forced upon me by fate or fear. My voice, once trembling and silent, now had the strength to express ideas, ask questions, and even share a bit of my creativity. My hands, once clenched nervously in my pockets, now placed posters on walls and offered to carry someone's load. My mind, once locked in a loop of what-ifs, now navigated uncertainty with a spirit of exploration.

As I neared the end of the notebook's first section, I read over my earlier entries. The contrast astonished me. The early pages spoke of fear, isolation, and an assumption that others would reject me. The later pages described small triumphs, growing empathy, and a newfound willingness to engage. I realized I had not merely recorded events; I had documented a transformation.

In that transformation, I found hope—not just for myself, but for anyone who feels lost. If I could evolve from silence to a quiet, determined voice, maybe others could too. Life still held many mysteries, and I was still a beginner in the art of understanding myself and others. Yet the journey no longer frightened me as it once had. Instead, it invited me forward with the promise that as long as I kept learning and growing, I would find new ways to connect, contribute, and find meaning.

With this understanding, I closed my notebook gently. Tomorrow would bring new challenges, but I would face them equipped with the insights and courage I had gained. My voice was my own, and though it might never be loud or perfect, it was honest and evolving. In that honesty, I discovered a quiet strength that would guide me as I continued walking through life's intricate paths.

6

Embracing the Wider Horizon

A faint scent of jasmine drifted through the air as I stepped outside one late afternoon, heading toward familiar streets that had once intimidated me. The sun was lower now, its glow softer than at midday, painting the world in warm hues. My pace was unhurried; I had no urgent errand, no pressing obligation—just a desire to see what might unfold if I allowed myself to wander with an open mind.

In the weeks since I'd begun taking those small, intentional steps—helping classmates, daring to speak in the reading circle, capturing my thoughts in a notebook—I'd grown more comfortable with uncertainty. My world now held more possibilities than threats. I looked at the uneven pavement, the crooked signboards, and the passing cyclists with a sense of familiarity and quiet fondness. This was my environment, once so daunting, now a place I could navigate with steadier footing.

I passed the roadside library stand again, nodding to the young man who managed it. He smiled back without surprise, as though expecting me. Today I didn't pause to pick a book. Instead, I simply enjoyed the reassurance of its presence, knowing I could browse whenever I wished. That small stand had once symbolized mystery and risk; now it represented comfort and growth.

While roaming, I found myself recalling a conversation I'd overheard at the reading circle. Two participants had discussed how people form communities not just through shared interests, but by supporting each other's growth. They'd mentioned that when individuals with different backgrounds and experiences come together, everyone benefits. At the time, I'd listened quietly, turning their words over in my mind. Now, as I considered my own journey—how the reading circle welcomed me, how classmates responded to my invitations, how the roadside shelf broadened my horizons—I realized I'd become part of multiple small communities woven into my daily life.

As I neared the temple courtyard, I noticed a poster announcing a "Cultural Exchange Evening." The event promised music, short readings, and informal talks by people from different neighborhoods. I felt a surge of interest. Attending would mean meeting unfamiliar faces and hearing unfamiliar voices. It might be challenging, but I'd learned that challenges often led to rewards. I made a mental note to come back the following evening, determined to see what I could learn from this gathering.

When I arrived at the courtyard the next evening, I found it more crowded than the reading circle gatherings. People milled about, chatting in small groups. A makeshift stage at one end displayed instruments and a microphone. I stood at the back, observing. My old habit, the desire to fade into invisibility, tugged at me. But this time, I resisted it. Instead, I reminded myself that I belonged here as much as anyone else, even if I had nothing prepared to share.

A moment later, someone tapped my shoulder. It was Ravi, the man from the reading circle, smiling warmly. "I'm glad you came," he said. "We have people from various communities performing tonight—songs, poetry, even a short storytelling session."

I returned his greeting, grateful for the familiar face. He introduced me to a few others, and I found myself engaged in small talk that no longer felt forced. They asked if I'd attended similar events, what I liked about reading, and whether I enjoyed the school's cultural day. Their questions were mild and genuine, and I answered honestly. Surprisingly, I realized I had opinions and experiences worth sharing. I mentioned how helping set up chairs at the school event made me appreciate behind-the-scenes efforts. One person nodded and said, "It's those quiet contributions that often matter most." I smiled at that—how far I'd come, from fearing even the simplest interaction to openly discussing my thoughts.

The evening's performances began. A woman sang a folk song that drew murmurs of appreciation from the crowd. A young man recited a poem in a language I didn't fully understand, yet the rhythm and emotion in his voice were captivating. Then a pair of students—older than me, perhaps in college—performed a brief dialogue about bridging cultural gaps. They weren't professional actors, but their sincerity shone through. The audience listened with quiet respect.

As I watched these performances, I realized something important: everyone on that stage took a risk. They stood before others, exposed their voices, their ideas, their art. Their courage mirrored my own smaller steps. Just as I had spoken in the reading circle or offered help to a classmate, they were choosing to share a piece of themselves. Some performers might have been nervous, yet their willingness to try created a space where others could learn and enjoy. Fear was present, but it did not rule the moment.

Near the end of the evening, Ravi mentioned that there would be an open-mic segment. Anyone who wished could come forward and share something brief—an anecdote, a thought, a quote. I felt my heart flutter again. Could I do that? I had spoken at the reading circle in a calmer setting, and I had read a simple poem there once. But this crowd was bigger, more varied. The idea was intimidating, yet enticing.

I'd learned that facing fear often led to growth, and I wanted to keep growing.

I scanned the crowd. Arun was there too, I noticed with a start. He stood chatting with a few people I didn't know, probably friends of friends. He caught my eye and waved. Had he come because I mentioned the reading circle and other events? The possibility made me feel less alone. Even if he hadn't, seeing a classmate here encouraged me—if he belonged, so did I.

Before I could overthink, I stepped forward when Ravi asked for volunteers. My pulse hammered in my ears, but I focused on my breathing. Reaching the small stage, I cleared my throat and introduced myself softly. "I don't have a poem or a song," I began, voice quivering slightly, "but I'd like to share something I've learned recently about facing fears." A hush settled, gentle and patient.

"I used to be very quiet," I said, glancing at the people who were waiting curiously. "I thought if I stayed silent, I would avoid mistakes and rejection. But I learned that by never speaking, I missed out on kindness and understanding that others were willing to offer. Bit by bit, I started talking—asking questions, helping out, sharing ideas. It was scary at first, but I realized I could survive small embarrassments, and many people were kinder than I expected."

I paused, gathering courage from the encouraging nods I saw. "I guess what I want to say is that everyone has fears, whether it's singing on stage or just talking to someone new. But when we face those fears, we create chances to learn about ourselves and others. That's made my world feel bigger, more welcoming."

My last sentence floated in the quiet air. For a moment, I worried I sounded naïve. Then, gentle applause broke out. It wasn't thunderous, but it was warm and real. A few people smiled; one even called out, "Well said!" My cheeks warmed with gratitude. Stepping down, I felt lighter than ever. I had spoken not just to strangers, but to a community that was willing to listen. My voice, once trembling and hidden, had carried a message that resonated with others.

After the event, as people drifted away, Arun approached me. "I didn't know you'd speak," he said, eyes bright with interest. "You sounded confident."

"Confident?" I almost laughed. "I was nervous. But maybe I'm learning that nervous and confident can coexist."

He nodded, thoughtful. "I think that's true. You've changed a lot since the beginning of the year. It's... nice to see."

A quiet pride stirred in me. Arun's words felt like confirmation of what I had sensed in my own reflections. Change was no longer a distant possibility; it was my lived reality. I had grown enough that others could notice.

Over the next week, I found that this experience at the cultural evening stayed with me like a gentle flame lighting my way. I felt less hesitant to strike up conversations, to discuss a class assignment, or to offer help without overanalyzing. Each interaction wasn't just a test of courage anymore—it was an opportunity to connect, learn, or simply exchange a kind word.

My notebook entries reflected this shift. I wrote about the cultural evening, describing how different performers dared to reveal something personal. I acknowledged that while I might never become a bold performer or a confident public speaker, I could engage with others in meaningful ways. Courage, I realized, wasn't limited to dramatic acts; it thrived in the mundane choices we made daily—to listen attentively, to speak honestly, to try something new even when uneasy.

I also noted something else: along this journey, I had gained more than skills or confidence. I'd developed a sense of purpose. Initially, I tried to overcome fear just to ease my isolation. Then I found joy in learning, connecting, and contributing. Now, I understood that using my voice and presence could help build a more supportive environment.

I wasn't merely fixing my problems; I was becoming a participant in something larger—a culture of understanding, where each person's efforts mattered.

Life still held challenges, of course. A few days later, a teacher corrected me sharply in class for misunderstanding instructions. I blushed, feeling old anxieties rise. But after class, instead of stewing in shame, I approached her to clarify where I went wrong. She explained patiently, and I thanked her. Previously, a scolding might have left me shaken for days; now, it was a brief setback, followed by a solution. I saw this resilience as yet another sign of my growth.

I also learned that I didn't need constant validation. Not everyone I reached out to had to respond warmly. Sometimes, people were busy, preoccupied, or simply not interested in conversation. I accepted that graciously, no longer interpreting silence or a brisk reply as a judgment of my worth. This emotional independence allowed me to keep engaging without the fear that one negative interaction would erase all my progress.

As more time passed, I began to consider my future steps. Perhaps I could join a small club at school or help organize another event. Maybe I could mentor someone younger who felt as lost as I once did, guiding them gently toward finding their own voice. The thought excited me—transforming my newfound capabilities into support for others. If I once benefited from empathetic listeners and encouraging words, I could now pass that on, continuing the cycle of understanding and growth.

Reflecting on all these changes, I recognized that growth is rarely linear. There were days I felt uncertain, when I preferred quiet observation over active participation. But I no longer saw that as failure. Silence could be comfortable, a time to recharge. The difference was that now silence was a choice, not a prison. I could choose when to speak and when to listen, and both choices felt equally valid.

I decided to celebrate my progress by revisiting the roadside library stand with a fresh perspective. This time, I would pick a book that challenged me—something more complex, maybe a collection of essays about human relationships or social change. When I found such a volume, I paged through it and discovered a chapter discussing how communities evolve over time, shaped by the small contributions of many individuals. Smiling to myself, I realized I was living proof of that idea. My tiny acts—asking a question, helping with an event, speaking at the open-mic—had not changed the world, but they had changed my world, and perhaps influenced it in subtle ways.

Returning the book to its place, I felt a sense of completeness. I had stepped beyond the narrow confines of fear and uncertainty and entered a space where learning, growing, and connecting felt natural. I saw no finish line, no final moment of triumph where I'd declare "I'm done improving." Instead, I embraced the ongoing nature of this journey. Each new experience, each conversation, each event would offer me another chance to refine my understanding and strengthen my moral compass.

As twilight approached, I wandered home, replaying the recent events in my mind: the reading circle's warmth, the cultural evening's courage, the notebook filled with insights. These experiences had woven together into a tapestry of personal evolution. I had shaped my voice by speaking truthfully, expressing empathy, and facing fears. And in return, I'd gained trust in my ability to navigate life's complexities.

No single chapter could capture the entirety of this transformation. But as I approached my home, I knew that I stood at the threshold of endless possibilities. The horizon had expanded, and I could walk toward it with open eyes and a steady heart, ready to contribute, learn, and discover whatever lay ahead.

IV

Integration Moral Reasoning into Adult Life

7

Walking Into the Wider World

A gentle rain tapped at the window as I sat at my desk, pen hovering over my open notebook. It was early evening, and the scent of damp earth drifted in through the cracks. Weeks had passed since the cultural exchange evening, and though my daily routines hadn't changed drastically—I still attended the same classes, walked the same streets, passed the same roadside library stand—my inner landscape felt markedly different.

I'd continued my quiet experiments: offering help when possible, asking questions without shame, and speaking up in group settings when I had something meaningful to say. Most people who knew me had adjusted to this new version of me—more engaged, more present, and more comfortable in my own skin. Even the teachers who once saw me as a silent figure now occasionally addressed me with a hint of encouragement, as if recognizing the potential I carried.

In my notebook, I tried to capture the subtle changes I'd noticed lately. I realized I was no longer just overcoming fear; I was starting to seek opportunities to grow and contribute. Months ago, stepping forward felt like a reckless gamble, a test of survival. Now, it felt natural, a way of life. I felt a stirring desire to take on something more sustained than simple, one-time acts. Something that would let me practice what I'd learned—cooperation, moral understanding, empathy—on a larger scale.

My thoughts drifted back to the reading circle and the cultural evening. Both had shown me the power of communities built around shared curiosity and respect. I wondered: could I help foster something similar in my own school environment, especially among my peers? Many students drifted through their days without discovering the joy of shared learning or supportive dialogue. What if I tried to create a small group—nothing grand, just a handful of classmates—who met regularly to discuss stories, reflect on moral dilemmas, or practice open communication?

The idea excited me, but I knew I had to approach it carefully. I couldn't just announce, "Let's start a discussion group!" and expect people to join. They might need a reason, a theme, or an activity that appealed to them. Something that felt relevant and worthwhile. I recalled how, at the reading circle, people shared short pieces of literature. Maybe I could invite a few classmates to read short stories and then talk about them—what they meant, how they related to our lives. It wouldn't have to be literary analysis in a formal sense—just honest conversations.

I decided to start small. The next day at school, I approached Arun—my classmate who had shown openness to trying new things—and shared my idea. We stood in a hallway between classes, students hurrying past in both directions.

"Arun," I said, voice low but calm, "I was thinking about forming a small group that meets maybe once a week after school. We'd pick a short story or an article and talk about it—what we think, what we feel, what it teaches us about life. Nothing formal, just a friendly exchange. Would you be interested?"

He tilted his head, considering. "That sounds interesting, actually.

It's different from what we usually do—just copying notes or talking about tests. I like the idea of a more open conversation."

Encouraged, I continued, "We don't have to force it. Even if it's just two or three of us, it might still be fun."

Arun nodded. "Count me in. I know a couple of others who might be curious. Maybe Priya—she loves reading—and Kamal, who's always asking big questions no one answers." He grinned. "This might give him a place to ask them."

Within a few days, we had gathered a small circle of five students: me, Arun, Priya (a thoughtful girl who often carried a book tucked under her arm), Kamal (a restless thinker, always probing for meaning), and Sana (soft-spoken, but keen to explore new ideas). After classes on a quiet Thursday, we met under a large peepal tree near the school's back field. The atmosphere felt informal, fresh. We had no desks, no chalkboards—just grass, tree roots, and each other's voices.

For our first discussion, I brought a short folk tale I'd found at the roadside library stand—a simple story about a traveler who, through small acts of kindness, changed the fate of a troubled village. I read it aloud, my voice steady, the words carried by a gentle breeze. Then we let silence settle before anyone spoke.

Priya broke it, "I like that it wasn't about a hero doing grand deeds. Just little kindnesses that, over time, shifted the villagers' attitudes."

Kamal nodded, fingers twitching with energy. "Exactly. It shows how small actions ripple out. It's like we're all connected by invisible threads. One kind gesture here might lead to another there."

Sana, who'd been leaning against the tree, said softly, "It makes me think about how I treat people daily. Maybe I underestimate how my words or gestures affect them."

Arun smiled. "That's the beauty of simple stories. They remind us that we have power, even if we don't feel powerful."

I listened, heart warm. This was what I'd hoped for: a space where we could practice empathy, moral reflection, and understanding without fear of judgment. No grades were at stake, no reputations on the line—just honest thinking and sharing. Over the next hour, we wove between the story's details and our own experiences, touching on times we'd received unexpected help or witnessed subtle changes in others due to small efforts. When we parted ways, I could sense a quiet exhilaration. We had created something meaningful out of thin air.

In the following weeks, we met regularly. Our group settled into a pattern: each session, someone brought a short text—sometimes a story, sometimes a newspaper article, sometimes a poem—and we'd read, reflect, and talk. The topics varied widely: a tale about forgiveness, a report on environmental care, a poem about loneliness. Each time, we discovered that literature and ideas gave us a safe arena to examine our own values. We learned to disagree politely, to listen deeply, and to link distant themes to our personal lives.

Our small circle also attracted curious glances. A few classmates passing by asked what we were doing, and occasionally someone would drop in for a session. Some never returned, finding it "too serious" or just not their thing, but a few stayed. Over time, we grew to about eight regular members. A teacher noticed our gatherings and, after a brief conversation, expressed support. She said, "It's rare to see students initiate their own intellectual community. Keep it up." Her encouragement meant a lot, reinforcing that we were on a valuable path.

Beyond the group, I continued navigating daily life with greater ease. I no longer saw teachers as distant authorities to be feared, but as experienced guides I could approach for clarification. I no longer saw classmates as potential sources of ridicule, but as individuals each dealing with their own complexities. This shift in perspective made school feel less like an arena of survival and more like a landscape of connections waiting to be cultivated.

However, growth seldom proceeds without challenges. As I became more confident and engaged, I encountered new dilemmas. One afternoon, I noticed a younger student, maybe in his first or second year at the school, being taunted by a couple of older boys near the sports field. They teased him about his clothes, his accent, and the way he fumbled with his bag's zipper. The younger boy tried to ignore them, face flushed, eyes downcast. My chest tightened. I remembered my own fears of judgment, how silence once seemed like the only refuge.

I hesitated, uncertain how to intervene. Should I speak up? What if the older boys turned on me? But I knew I couldn't just walk away. The morals I'd been exploring in our discussions demanded action. If I believed in kindness and empathy, I had to live them, not just talk about them.

Steeling myself, I approached. Keeping my voice calm and steady, I said, "Hey, is there a reason you're bothering him?" The older boys looked at me, surprised. They hadn't expected an interruption. I could feel my heart pounding, but I maintained eye contact.

"Who are you?" one scoffed, but not too aggressively.

I shrugged. "Just someone who thinks this isn't right. He's not bothering you, so why pick on him?"

The younger student glanced up, hope flickering in his eyes. The older boys exchanged looks—maybe they were weighing if it was worth escalating. After a tense moment, one muttered something under his breath, and they walked away, leaving the younger boy behind. I turned to him and asked, "You okay?"

He nodded, voice trembling, "Yes. Thank you."

I smiled. "You shouldn't have to deal with that. Keep your head up." As I walked away, I felt a complex mix of relief and pride. I'd faced down a lingering fear—the fear of confrontation—and chosen to protect someone more vulnerable. This didn't make me a hero, I knew, but it was a step toward being consistent with the values I cherished.

Moral growth meant applying understanding in challenging moments, not just in friendly discussions under a tree.

That evening, I wrote about the incident in my notebook, reflecting on courage. I realized courage wasn't limited to performing in front of a crowd or asking questions in class. Sometimes it was standing up for someone else, even when uncertain of the outcome. This expanded my understanding of morality once more, showing me that empathy and integrity must sometimes manifest as direct intervention.

As our small reading-and-discussion group continued, we ventured into more nuanced topics. Priya brought a story about cultural misunderstandings, and we debated how easily people form stereotypes when they fail to communicate openly. Kamal found an article on ethical dilemmas in technology—how inventions meant for good could be misused. These discussions challenged us to think beyond personal interactions, nudging us to consider societal issues. I was impressed by how even a small group of teenagers could tackle such complexities with earnest effort.

Interestingly, we discovered that the more we practiced discussing moral and social questions, the more confident we became in expressing ourselves elsewhere. Sana, who used to speak barely above a whisper, grew bolder in giving her opinions. Arun, who was generally laid-back, sometimes challenged us with hard questions, forcing us to dig deeper. I noticed that even outside the group, we tried to reason more calmly about conflicts. The skills we cultivated here—listening, empathizing, analyzing—spilled into the rest of our lives.

Not all discussions went smoothly. Sometimes we disagreed strongly. One afternoon, Kamal and Priya argued over whether it was ever justified to lie for a noble cause. Kamal insisted that honesty was paramount, while Priya pointed out situations in which withholding a harmful truth could prevent suffering. The debate grew heated, voices rising. I worried that this might fracture our harmony. But before it got out of hand, Sana spoke up: "Isn't the point of this group to explore complexity rather than pretend we have all the answers?"

We paused, her gentle reminder washing over us. We realized that disagreement was not a failure; it was an opportunity to understand different moral perspectives. This insight calmed us. We ended the session acknowledging that we might not reach a consensus, but we had all learned from the exchange. Accepting uncertainty and maintaining respect became another cornerstone of our evolving culture.

As time passed, word of our group reached a teacher who taught literature and social studies. Curious, she asked if we'd consider helping organize a small school event—maybe a "debate and dialogue" session or a mini-exhibition of student reflections. The idea thrilled me. This was a chance to extend what we'd created, to invite more students into meaningful conversations. I shared the teacher's suggestion with the group, and while some were nervous about going public, we agreed it could be worthwhile. We decided to host a small "Idea Exchange Day" in a few weeks, open to anyone interested.

Preparing for this event challenged us on a new level. We had to pick a theme: something broad enough to interest many, yet specific enough to foster real conversation. After much deliberation, we settled on "Everyday Ethics: How Our Daily Choices Shape Our World." It felt relevant and accessible. Everyone made daily choices—how to treat classmates, what to consume, how to respond to conflict—and these choices had moral weight, even if we rarely acknowledged it.

We planned activities: a short panel discussion where a few volunteers would share personal stories about times they'd struggled with moral decisions; a "reflection wall" where students could write anonymous notes about a moral question that puzzled them; and small group discussions like the ones we held under the tree, but now in a more open setting. We asked the supportive teacher if we could use the school's assembly hall. She agreed, seeing educational value in our efforts.

The weeks leading up to the Idea Exchange Day were hectic. We designed simple posters, pinned them on bulletin boards, and spread the word through classmates. Some responded with enthusiasm—"Finally, something different from the usual sports or academic events!"—while others were skeptical, saying it sounded too "serious" or "boring." I tried not to be discouraged. If even a fraction of the students came and found value, that would be enough.

On the morning of the event, I arrived early with Arun and Priya to arrange chairs and set up a table with blank papers and markers for the reflection wall. My stomach fluttered. I recalled the nervousness I'd felt when first speaking at the reading circle or on stage at the cultural evening. This was a bigger stage, metaphorically—our peers would see what we were doing. But I reminded myself of how far I'd come. Nerves and confidence could coexist, as I'd told Arun. The goal was not to impress everyone, but to create a space for honest conversation.

When the time came, students trickled in. Some hovered by the door, unsure if they should enter, but curiosity often prevailed. We started with a short introduction, explaining that this wasn't about right or wrong answers, but about exploring everyday moral dimensions. Arun shared how reading a simple folk tale had changed his perspective on kindness. Sana spoke briefly about her initial shyness and how talking openly about values helped her grow stronger in her convictions. I mentioned the younger student I'd defended, showing that moral courage could appear in unexpected places.

The "reflection wall" idea surprised me with its effectiveness. Students wrote questions and stuck them up: "Is it okay to prioritize my friends' comfort over being honest?" "How do I handle pressure to behave cruelly in a group?" "Why do I feel guilty when I waste resources, but I do it anyway?" These questions revealed that many struggled quietly with moral uncertainties. Seeing them displayed publicly validated these struggles, showing we weren't alone in our confusion.

We then split into small groups, each facilitated by one of our reading-group members. I guided a group of six students who were initially shy. We picked one of the posted questions: "How do we remain kind when we're angry at someone?" Initially, no one spoke. I remembered my early silence and decided to lead by example. I said, "I've felt that way many times. Anger makes me want to lash out, but I learned if I pause and remember that the other person is human, with reasons and pains I may not know, it's harder to stay cruel." This opened the door. Another student said he sometimes wrote down his feelings before confronting a friend who upset him, so he wouldn't speak in anger. Another mentioned imagining how they'd feel if someone treated them harshly.

As we talked, I could see the tension in their shoulders easing. They realized anger didn't have to lead to cruelty; it could be acknowledged, understood, and channeled more productively. We didn't solve every issue, but we shared strategies and perspectives. This was the essence of what I'd dreamed of: a community of learners, practicing moral reasoning as a lived skill, not an abstract concept.

Across the hall, I saw Kamal's group animatedly discussing resource waste and consumer choices. Priya's group handled dilemmas about loyalty and honesty. Arun's group tackled peer pressure to insult or exclude others. Sana quietly guided her group, ensuring everyone spoke at least once. The atmosphere hummed with engagement. Students who rarely raised their hand in class now shared personal anecdotes. Laughter and solemn nods mixed freely. The Idea Exchange Day felt like a small miracle: we had offered a platform, and our peers responded with openness and courage.

After about an hour and a half, we reconvened. I stood at the front, scanning faces. They looked thoughtful, some still uncertain, but I sensed they'd found value in the process. "We might not leave here with firm answers," I said, "but we've seen that our everyday choices matter, and that talking about them helps. We've proven we're capable of respectful dialogue, and that's a strength we can carry forward."

Applause followed—modest, but heartfelt. A teacher approached me afterward and said, "I'm impressed. You've shown your classmates that moral thinking isn't just for philosophers—it's for everyone."

As people drifted out, a girl I didn't know well tapped my arm. "I never realized others worried about the same moral issues as I do," she said quietly. "I feel less alone now." Her words stayed with me, reaffirming that even if only a few gained insight, we had succeeded.

In the following days, life returned to normal rhythms—classes, homework, chatter in hallways—but a subtle shift lingered. Those who attended the event sometimes referred back to it. "This reminds me of that question we discussed," someone would say when facing a small moral dilemma. Our reading group continued meeting under the tree, proud that we'd sparked a broader conversation.

I reflected more deeply: what had all this taught me about morality, growth, and community? I realized that morality thrives in relationships. Alone, I might overthink and fear making mistakes, but in dialogue, I discover that others share my uncertainties and can help me see them differently. Morality also thrives in action. By defending that younger student, organizing the Idea Exchange Day, and consistently practicing empathy, I reinforced my moral identity, turning abstract values into lived realities.

Moreover, I learned that being a good listener was as important as being a good speaker. Initially, I focused on overcoming silence to express myself. Now I understood that listening gave me access to multiple viewpoints, making me wiser and less prone to assuming my perspective was the only valid one. This humility was a precious gift.

As weeks turned into months, I wondered how these experiences would shape my future. One day I'd leave this school, meet new people, face new challenges. But the skills and values I nurtured here—openness, empathy, courage, and moral reflection—would travel with me. Just as reading had opened my mind, living ethically would open my heart. I could walk into wider worlds without feeling overwhelmed by their complexity.

I also noticed that my initial fear of judgment had faded significantly. I no longer worried incessantly about appearing foolish. After all, I had dared to speak publicly about my fears and learned that vulnerability often earns respect rather than ridicule. In fact, I now saw vulnerability as a bridge connecting people's inner worlds. When we admitted uncertainty or acknowledged mistakes, we invited others to do the same, forging mutual understanding.

In the hallway one afternoon, I overheard a conversation between two classmates who hadn't joined our sessions or events. They discussed a minor conflict they'd had with a friend. To my surprise, one said, "Maybe we should try seeing it from her point of view." The other nodded. It struck me that perhaps the idea of empathy was spreading indirectly. Even those who didn't attend the event might have heard snippets or felt the shift in our school's atmosphere. It was a gentle reminder that cultural change can begin with small sparks.

Reflecting on my personal journey, I realized something crucial: I had not climbed a ladder that ended at a summit of moral perfection. Instead, I had learned to navigate moral terrain with more confidence and curiosity. I accepted that I would still stumble, encounter new fears, and face ethical puzzles I couldn't easily solve. But now I saw those difficulties as invitations to learn, not as threats to my worth.

My notebook entries became less frantic, less focused on fear, and more exploratory. I wrote about the interplay between self-interest and altruism, about how acknowledging one's imperfections can make moral growth more accessible. I considered questions like: Do we owe kindness to strangers? How do we balance honesty with compassion? Each page filled with thoughts and questions, not definitive answers, reflecting my comfort with uncertainty.

Our reading group also evolved. We tried new formats—role-playing scenarios, discussing brief news headlines, comparing personal stories from different cultural backgrounds. Some members came and went, but a core remained, committed to this collective exploration. Through all these activities, we learned that moral understanding was not a static lesson to be memorized but an ongoing conversation enriched by diverse voices.

I also revisited the reading circle at the temple courtyard more often. Listening to older community members, I gained perspectives on moral challenges that extended beyond the school environment. They talked about struggles in workplaces, families, and neighborhoods, showing me that moral reasoning is a lifelong skill, not something confined to youth or education. Their humility reminded me that growing older doesn't guarantee moral clarity—one must stay attentive and reflective.

Encouraged by these insights, I considered how I might continue contributing to my community. Perhaps I could volunteer for a local library reading session or help a younger student group form their own discussion circle. Maybe, in time, I could write something—an article or a short guide—sharing what I'd learned about starting dialogues on moral issues among peers. The possibilities felt endless, not burdensome.

One morning, while passing the sports field, I recognized the younger boy I'd once protected from bullies. He was playing catch with a friend, smiling easily. He no longer looked frightened or withdrawn. I hoped, in my small intervention, I had made a positive difference. The memory reminded me that sometimes, moral courage's impact is subtle and long-lasting, even if we never get formal acknowledgment.

As the school year neared its end, exams and future plans hovered in everyone's minds. Amid the academic stress, I noticed that the friendships I'd formed or deepened through moral conversations provided emotional support. When worried about a test, I could talk to my reading-group peers and receive understanding instead of empty platitudes. We had learned to communicate beyond superficial topics—our bond was more resilient.

On the last day of formal classes, before exams started, our group met one final time under the peepal tree. We knew we'd be busy revising soon, and our gatherings might pause until the break. We didn't have a text to discuss this time. Instead, we reflected on what we'd gained from these sessions. Arun spoke of increased confidence in voicing concerns. Priya said she saw stories not just as entertainment but as windows into moral worlds. Kamal admitted he learned to respect viewpoints different from his own intellectual stances. Sana said she now felt her voice mattered, and that moral reflection didn't require loudness, just honesty.

They asked me what I'd gained. I took a moment to answer, eyes following a crow swooping overhead. "I've learned that we all have moral potential. Fear and silence don't make us safer; they limit our growth. By risking communication, we discover empathy, and with empathy, we find collective wisdom. I've learned that morality is not a burden but a shared endeavor that enriches our lives."

We lingered after that, comfortable in silence, the sun's rays filtering through leaves. The moment felt like a quiet culmination. I knew life would continue to challenge us, and we might disperse into different paths one day. But the lessons and bonds formed here would travel with us.

The final weeks of school flew by. I focused on exams, applying the same calm reasoning I'd learned to apply to moral questions. When anxious thoughts arose—what if I fail, what if I don't meet expectations—I remembered that I had faced much scarier inner battles and emerged stronger. This perspective allowed me to approach tests not as threats but as tasks. My performance improved naturally, because I approached learning with curiosity rather than fear.

After the last exam, as students prepared to leave for the vacation, I felt a bittersweet mix of pride and melancholy. Change was ongoing. Some classmates would move to other schools, some would stay. The reading group might evolve or reform next term in another shape. The Idea Exchange Day would be a memory, but maybe others would take inspiration and organize their own events. I had to trust that the seeds we planted would grow in ways we might never fully see.

Before parting, I gifted my notebook to myself, wrapping it in a simple cloth and putting it away safely. It contained a record of my transformation, from silent fear to a voice shaped by dialogue and moral engagement. I wanted to preserve those words, to revisit them in the future when faced with new dilemmas, reminding myself of the journey I had already taken.

On my way out of the school gates, I stopped by the roadside library stand one last time. The young man was rearranging books. I thanked him for keeping this informal library running. He looked up, puzzled. "I didn't do much," he said. "I just put books here."

"Sometimes small acts make a big difference," I replied. "Your books started a chain of events for me." He smiled, still a bit puzzled, but nodded. I walked away, grateful for how unexpected sources—a shelf of books, a reading circle, a few curious peers—had guided me toward a richer moral understanding.

The sky was overcast, yet I sensed brightness within myself. I knew I was not finished learning. The world remained vast and complicated, full of moral trials. But now I had tools: empathy, dialogue, courage, reflection. With these, I could navigate complexities without freezing in fear or cynicism. Instead of feeling trapped, I felt free to explore moral landscapes with curiosity.

As I stepped into the wider world beyond the school's boundaries, I embraced the journey ahead. My life's path would likely offer new challenges—relationships to nurture, injustices to address, mistakes to rectify, ambitions to clarify. In all these contexts, the moral reasoning I'd practiced would serve as a compass. It wouldn't provide absolute answers, but it would guide me to ask better questions, seek understanding before judgment, and value kindness over dominance.

I realized that moral growth is not a state you achieve and hold forever; it's a continuous process. Every new situation invites a choice: Will I act with integrity or fear? Will I listen deeply or shut down? Will I learn or stagnate? Each time I chose growth, I would strengthen my moral muscles. Each time I stumbled, I could get up, learn from the fall, and continue forward.

The protagonist in my first folk tale reading had changed a village with small acts of kindness. I hadn't changed a whole village, but I'd contributed to my school's culture, influenced friendships, and shaped my own destiny. That was enough proof that individuals can make a difference in their spheres, however modest. Over time, these spheres interconnect, creating ripples across communities and generations.

In my pocket, I carried a small folded paper from the reflection wall at the Idea Exchange Day. On it, someone had written: "Why is it so hard to be kind when the world seems harsh?" I kept it as a reminder that moral questions never vanish. They persist, challenging each new generation. But I also kept it to remember that I was not alone in wrestling with them. Others asked the same questions, felt the same struggles, and by coming together, we alleviated the burden.

Walking down a quiet street, I imagined my future self looking back on these days. Perhaps I'd smile at my younger fear, proud of how I overcame it. Perhaps I'd recall the faces of those who joined our discussions under the tree, grateful for their influence on my growth. Perhaps I'd still write in a notebook, processing new moral puzzles as they arose.

Rain began to fall more steadily, each drop a tiny note of renewal. I didn't seek shelter immediately. Instead, I allowed the rain to wash over me, cooling my skin, baptizing me into the next phase of life. The fear that once gripped me had dissolved into a calmer understanding that I could handle complexity. Morality, I'd learned, is an art of living that demands creativity and collaboration, not dogma or perfection.

With these thoughts, I turned a corner and disappeared from the familiar school surroundings, stepping forward into the unknown with steady steps, a compassionate heart, and a mind prepared to learn endlessly.

8

Expanding the Circle of Influence

A dry, warm breeze brushed my face as I stepped off the bus into a bustling street. Months had passed since I left the familiar world of school corridors and reading circles under a peepal tree. Life had moved steadily on: I'd completed my secondary education, taken some time to consider my future, and decided to enroll in a nearby college. It wasn't too far from home—just a short bus ride each day—but it felt like a different universe. The crowds were larger, the pace faster, and the expectations less defined. No one at the college knew me yet, knew what I'd achieved or how I'd grown. I arrived as an unknown, a blank slate.

As I navigated the college campus on my first day, I recalled how nervous I'd once been about simply speaking in front of classmates. Now, though excitement and curiosity hummed in my veins, I felt more grounded. I understood that fear might still arise, but I had faced bigger challenges before and learned to welcome uncertainty rather than dread it. I had a moral compass shaped by honest dialogue and empathy, and this gave me quiet confidence. A new environment meant new chances to learn and contribute.

The college itself was an older building with wide corridors and worn stone steps. Students milled around in groups, talking and laughing in several languages, their clothing and styles more varied than in my old school. Some looked rushed, heads bent over phones; others lounged casually, as if they had all the time in the world. The diversity of attitudes and backgrounds intrigued me. Back in school, we had a relatively uniform community, but here the mosaic was richer.

My initial days were spent finding classrooms, meeting professors, and introducing myself to classmates who greeted me with polite nods or friendly smiles. I listened more than I spoke at first, mapping the social terrain. Who seemed approachable? Who was locked in their own concerns? I watched for subtle cues: the student who paused to hold a door for a stranger, the one who muttered impatiently when the canteen line moved slowly. Moral behavior revealed itself in small gestures here too. The college, like my old school, was made of individuals with their own uncertainties and hopes.

One afternoon, sitting under a neem tree near the library, I found myself recalling the reading circle I once fostered. Could I create something similar here? The idea tempted me—an informal group to discuss ideas, moral issues, and stories—yet I knew college students might have different priorities. Some might consider deep conversations a luxury they couldn't afford, juggling part-time jobs or family responsibilities. Others might be intrigued, hungry for more meaning than lectures and exams could offer. I decided to keep the idea in mind, waiting for the right moment or the right people to appear.

In the meantime, I immersed myself in my courses. I took subjects that broadened my perspective: literature from various cultures, a sociology course examining social structures, and a philosophy class introducing me to thinkers who had grappled with moral questions centuries ago. Sitting in those lectures, I found echoes of the dialogues I'd held under the peepal tree. Philosophers like Aristotle or Confucius might have seemed distant, but their concerns about virtue, kindness, and justice resonated with what my small school group had discovered empirically.

Outside of class, I explored the campus clubs. There were groups for debating, environmental activism, theater, music, and many more. Joining a club might help me find like-minded individuals. Eventually, I drifted towards a small "Community Service Collective" that advertised weekend visits to local NGOs, tutoring underprivileged children, and neighborhood clean-up drives. The description reminded me of the values I cherished: empathy, responsibility, and practical action. I signed up, hopeful that this would help me connect my moral understanding to real-world impact.

The first meeting of the Community Service Collective took place in a quiet corner of the college canteen. About ten people showed up: some older students who had run the group for years, and a handful of newcomers like me. The leaders, Sahana and Dev, greeted us warmly and explained their current projects. Sahana, a calm, thoughtful person, described how they volunteered at a children's shelter every Saturday, helping kids with basic reading and writing skills. Dev, more energetic, mentioned environmental clean-ups and working with local elders in a community center.

They asked what motivated us newcomers to join. Some cited a desire to "give back" or to improve their resumes, while others felt curiosity. When my turn came, I said quietly, "I've learned that discussing moral issues and practicing empathy in daily life matters. I'm here to find ways to apply those values—help people, address small injustices, and keep learning from real experiences." Sahana nodded, a flicker of understanding in her eyes.

Over the next weeks, I participated in a few service activities. We visited the children's shelter on a Saturday morning. The kids were shy at first, but warmed up after we introduced a simple storybook and read aloud. Their eyes sparkled at the tale's adventures. I remembered the power of stories—how they once helped my classmates and me explore moral choices. Here, stories could inspire children and unlock their imagination. After reading, we asked them what they learned. Their answers were honest and unfiltered: "It's good to help a friend," "Don't be mean to people who look different," and "Sharing makes everyone happy." They proved that moral insights were accessible even to the very young.

This volunteering revived feelings I had at school—how small acts could shape attitudes, how meeting others halfway bridged differences. Yet it also presented new complexities. Some children faced harsh circumstances at home. Their struggles hinted that kindness alone wasn't enough; social and economic factors weighed heavily on their lives. Morality here extended beyond personal choices to systemic issues. I felt humbled. The world was bigger and more complicated than a single group discussion could capture, and I realized I needed to integrate moral reasoning with an understanding of social realities.

I began discussing these thoughts with Sahana after the volunteering sessions. She listened attentively. "You're right," she said. "It's not just about telling kids to be kind; we must also recognize the structures that limit their opportunities. But still, offering them support and positive experiences matters. It's one piece of a larger puzzle."

I appreciated her balanced perspective. She reminded me of how in my old reading group we acknowledged uncertainty and complexity. Here, too, we had to accept that no single action solved everything, but each sincere effort helped.

As I spent more time in college, I grew comfortable with its rhythms. I formed a small circle of friends from various backgrounds: Arjun, a first-generation college student passionate about politics; Leila, who studied psychology and loved analyzing why people behaved the way they did; and Jose, a quiet observer who spoke thoughtfully when he finally did speak. Over lunch breaks, we sometimes dipped into moral questions without labeling them as such—discussing a news story about corruption or a debate about whether the college should divest from companies harming the environment.

One day, Leila mentioned a student in one of her classes who openly mocked people from a certain community. "It's frustrating," she said, "He uses stereotypes as if it's a joke. How should we respond? Ignore him or confront him?" This dilemma reminded me of the bullies I'd once stopped at school. But we were older now, and such prejudice might run deeper. Arjun suggested we should call him out publicly. Jose said maybe we should talk to him privately, understand where he's coming from. I found myself leaning towards a balanced approach—first trying a private conversation to humanize the victims of his jokes, and if that failed, standing up publicly. We didn't reach a consensus, but the conversation itself had value. Again, I saw how moral reasoning thrived in dialogue.

As my comfort grew, I returned to the idea of forming a discussion group like the one I had in school. I mentioned it casually to Arjun and Leila. "Something simple: reading a short story or an article and discussing what it says about how we treat each other. No grades, no pressure, just exploration."

Arjun shrugged. "Might be interesting, but people here have busy schedules. You'll need a good hook."

Leila added, "Maybe start small—invite a few people you trust, see if it grows. Also, pick materials that relate to college life: dealing with competition, cultural misunderstandings, or balancing personal ambition with ethical standards."

This was sound advice. After some thought, I chose a short article discussing "everyday moral compromises"—like copying notes from a friend without attributing them, or taking more than your fair share of communal resources. These issues were tangible to college students. I invited Arjun, Leila, and Jose, along with Sahana from the service collective, and Dev as well, to a casual evening meet-up near the library lawn. I told them to bring anyone who might be interested.

On the appointed evening, I set out a few printouts of the article under a large banyan tree on campus. About seven people showed up—more than I expected. Sahana and Dev brought a friend each, and Jose convinced one of his quiet classmates to join. I introduced the concept just as I had done years ago: "This is a space to think out loud about moral issues that shape our daily lives. We'll read something short and then share thoughts. No one's an expert; we're all learning."

We read the article, which detailed small moral slips—fudging a report, grabbing extra stationery from the supply room, or speaking politely to someone while harboring resentment. The discussion started slowly, as people tested the waters. Then Dev mentioned how he felt conflicted when asked by a friend to share notes from a class the friend never attended. Was it kindness or enabling irresponsibility? Sahana countered that sometimes people have genuine reasons for missing classes and need help. Arjun said he hated the idea of enabling laziness, but also didn't want to deny help if it might make a real difference. The debate warmed up, branching into questions of trust, fairness, and compassion.

Listening to these college peers dissect everyday morality reminded me of my old school group. The spirit was similar: respectful exploration, accepting that no perfect solution existed, but we could sharpen each other's understanding. Leila pointed out that we often rationalize minor wrongdoings, and maybe discussions like this help us catch ourselves. Jose suggested that even if we don't find one rule to follow, being aware of the moral dimensions improves our decision-making.

The session ended with people looking thoughtful. Sahana said, "I never knew it could be so interesting to dissect these small moral choices. We usually ignore them, assuming they're trivial." One of the newcomers asked if we'd do this again. I nodded, smiling. It seemed we had planted another seed—a new moral inquiry group adapting to the college's context.

Over the following months, these gatherings became semi-regular. We tried different formats—sometimes a poem or a snippet from a philosopher's work, sometimes a scenario one of us faced. The group fluctuated in size, but a core of five or six remained steady. Occasionally, fresh faces popped in, intrigued by rumor of "that ethics chat group under the banyan tree." Some left unimpressed or too busy, but others stayed, enjoying the mental exercise and the sense of community.

I noticed that as we engaged more deeply, people brought in experiences from their volunteer work, classes, and personal challenges. Dev recounted a moral quandary: while cleaning up a neighborhood, he discovered some residents resented our presence, seeing it as showy charity rather than genuine help. How to address their concerns respectfully while maintaining our purpose? We discussed approaching them to understand their perspective, acknowledging their pride and independence, and maybe collaborating with them rather than imposing solutions. Once again, moral reasoning meant seeking empathy, listening, and adapting.

Life's complexities continued to emerge. I found myself wrestling with bigger issues: how does one navigate the college's competitive environment without losing sight of moral values like honesty and solidarity? Is it wrong to push oneself too hard at the expense of personal well-being? Our group tackled such questions too. We explored the tension between ambition and ethics. Leila, studying psychology, contributed insights about how stress and fear influence our moral choices. Arjun, more politically minded, warned that personal morality must also engage with systemic inequalities—no matter how kind we are as individuals, we should not ignore broader injustices.

Hearing these perspectives enriched my understanding. In my old school circle, we dealt mostly with interpersonal kindness and respect. Now, I saw morality as layered: personal interactions, institutional frameworks, cultural narratives, and global issues all intertwined. The complexity could feel overwhelming, but I reminded myself that moral reasoning does not promise final answers. It teaches us to navigate with humility and compassion.

One incident challenged me personally. I discovered that a friend, Jose, had unintentionally hurt another student's feelings by making a sarcastic remark about their project. It happened in a group setting, and the student left abruptly, clearly upset. Jose shrugged it off initially, but I felt bothered. Should I say something to Jose? He was a friend, and I knew he meant no real harm, but his words had been careless. I wrestled internally, recalling how speaking up at school helped prevent harm. If I said nothing, I might be allowing a culture of casual disrespect to fester.

Gathering my courage, I approached Jose in private. "I wanted to talk about something," I began, choosing my words carefully. "At that group meeting, your comment about that student's project seemed to upset them. I know you're not a cruel person, but maybe we should consider how our humor affects others."

Jose looked surprised and a bit defensive. "I was just joking. He's too sensitive," he said.

I took a breath, remembering that moral persuasion needed empathy. "I understand it was a joke, but jokes can still hurt, especially if someone's invested in what they're doing. We've been talking in our sessions about respecting others' efforts. Maybe this is a chance to align our actions with our words."

He hesitated, then sighed. "I guess I didn't think about it from his perspective. Maybe I should apologize."

My heart lightened. Jose's willingness to reconsider proved that these moral discussions had not been abstract. They equipped us to call each other in, not just call out. The next day, he found the student and offered a sincere apology. The student accepted, relieved. This small resolution reaffirmed that moral growth is a continuous process, sustained by caring confrontation and reflection.

As the semester advanced, our circle under the banyan tree tackled even more profound themes. Someone brought an article about global injustice—migrant crises, wealth gaps, environmental degradation. We debated what responsibility we, as students, bore for problems that seemed enormous and distant. Arjun argued that we must engage politically, push for systemic change. Leila said personal choices, like consuming responsibly and supporting fair initiatives, also matter. Dev noted that volunteering locally, though limited, builds skills and empathy that might scale up later. I realized our discussions had matured. We were no longer just pondering daily niceties; we were asking how to live morally in a flawed world.

The weight of these issues sometimes felt heavy. Could we really make a difference? Sahana reminded us that grand solutions might elude us, but engaging in the moral conversation was itself valuable. It kept us open to learning and prevented numbness in the face of suffering. I recalled how at school, acknowledging complexity didn't paralyze us; it inspired careful action.

Outside the discussion group and service collective, I continued volunteering with the children's shelter. Over time, I got to know some kids by name. One girl, Rina, struggled with reading. I spent extra time helping her form letters and words. Seeing her improvement and growing confidence touched me deeply. It reminded me that moral thinking and compassion shouldn't remain theoretical. Small, steady acts of support, repeated over time, could transform someone's world—even if just a bit.

Rina's struggles also taught me patience. When she stumbled over the same letter multiple times, I felt tempted to give up or grow frustrated. But I remembered how easily frustration can undermine kindness. Patience itself was a moral choice—valuing her dignity and right to learn at her own pace. Eventually, she read a short sentence flawlessly, beaming with pride. In that moment, all the moral theorizing we did under the banyan tree crystallized into a tangible outcome: one child realizing she could read and therefore learn, grow, and imagine more.

As the semester neared its end, I reflected on my journey. I had replicated, in a new environment, the essence of what I discovered in school. Dialogue, empathy, and moral inquiry worked not only with my old classmates but also with new, diverse peers. The seeds of moral reasoning, once planted under a peepal tree, had sprouted under a banyan tree, nourished by a different community. This continuity reassured me that the moral growth process I underwent in school was not a one-time event, but a skill set I could carry anywhere.

Another realization struck me: just as I had guided Rina, others had guided me. The old reading circle at school, my college mentors, Sahana's balanced counsel, the philosophers I read, the children's direct moral simplicity—all had shaped my evolving perspective. Moral growth was communal, collaborative. I had influenced others, like Jose, and they had influenced me. We formed a network of moral relationships, each reinforcing the others.

Toward the end of the academic year, our banyan tree group decided to host a small event—less formal than the school's Idea Exchange Day, but similar in spirit. We called it "Moral Moments: Stories of Everyday Choices." Everyone would bring a short anecdote, a personal experience where they confronted a moral dilemma, big or small. We hoped to draw a few curious students and maybe spark broader interest, just as I had done before.

On a mild evening, about twelve people gathered, some familiar, some new. We arranged ourselves in a loose circle on the grass. I started by sharing a recent struggle: debating whether to report a classmate who I suspected was plagiarizing. I explained how I weighed loyalty, justice, and the potential consequences for him. In the end, I chose to approach him privately, giving him a chance to correct his path before taking harsher steps. He admitted his mistake, promised to rewrite his assignment honestly. I still wondered if I did the right thing, but at least I tried dialogue before punishment.

Others shared their stories: Arjun recounted intervening when someone spread rumors. Leila described her inner battle to maintain humility after receiving praise for a project. Dev talked about his conflict between taking on more volunteer responsibilities and risking burnout. Each anecdote revealed that morality lived not in grand declarations, but in the subtle tensions of daily life, where values collided and needed careful navigation.

The new attendees listened intently. One of them, an older student close to graduation, commented, "I've walked these corridors for years and never thought to hold such a discussion. It's refreshing to hear peers openly acknowledging uncertainty." Another first-year student said, "I always thought morality was about big issues like crime or politics. Now I see it's also about how we treat classmates, handle group assignments, and manage stress."

Their responses warmed me. It showed that the moral inquiry we fostered could resonate with people at different stages, reminding them that ethics belonged not just in philosophy textbooks but in everyday choices. After the event, several people lingered, discussing ways to keep moral reflection alive on campus. Some suggested collaborating with the debate club or writing a column in the student newsletter about ethical dilemmas. Others wanted to merge with cultural clubs, using art and stories to spark moral conversations.

As I walked home under a fading sky, I felt a quiet sense of fulfillment. My initial fear in school had led me to discover moral dialogue as a tool for personal and communal growth. Now, in college, I had confirmed that this approach was portable, adaptable, and beneficial. Moral discourse didn't solve all problems, but it enriched minds, connected hearts, and encouraged thoughtful action.

I also contemplated my future beyond college. Would I carry these lessons into a workplace, a family setting, or a civic environment? Very likely, yes. The world, as I'd repeatedly learned, offered no shortage of moral tests. Interpersonal kindness, integrity in professional matters, political engagement, and cultural understanding would all test my moral compass again and again. But I welcomed these tests, knowing I had a method: reflect, dialogue, empathize, and act with courage.

A few days later, I bumped into Sahana on campus. We walked together toward the bus stop, reflecting on the year's journey. "It's amazing how a few discussions can shift people's perspectives," she said, smiling. "I've seen newcomers become more thoughtful, more willing to consider consequences."

"True," I replied. "And I've learned to appreciate that moral development isn't linear. We expand our understanding step by step, influenced by each conversation, each encounter."

She nodded. "That's growth. We don't arrive at a final moral code; we just keep refining how we live and relate to others."

Her words echoed my deepest conclusion. Morality was not a checklist of rules to master and be done with. It was a practice, an art, evolving as we matured and faced new conditions. Each environment—school, college, future workplaces—offered fresh moral landscapes to navigate. Each relationship brought new lessons. Instead of seeking a static ideal, I embraced the dynamic process of becoming more morally aware, more empathetic, and more effective at doing good.

That evening, I opened my notebook—the one I had started fresh in college—and found pages filled with questions, reflections from our tree discussions, and notes from our service activities. Reading through them, I saw a record of evolving complexity: early entries focused on personal fears and interpersonal kindness; later ones grappled with systemic issues, ethical dilemmas in resource allocation, the balance between honesty and compassion. The progression comforted me. It signaled continuous learning and adjusting.

My mind drifted back to the younger me standing silently in a school corridor, too afraid to speak. How much had changed since then! Now I led discussions, engaged in volunteer work, confronted friends about hurtful jokes, and considered global injustices. Fear had not vanished, but it had lost its dominance. I understood that fear signaled a chance to be courageous, to learn something new. Each moral dilemma was no longer a threat, but a puzzle inviting collective reasoning.

In the final week before summer break, the college halls grew quieter. Many students left early. I stayed a bit longer, settling some library dues and helping Sahana and Dev plan future service activities. We drafted a tentative schedule for the next semester: visiting another local community center, organizing a small workshop on cultural sensitivity, and maybe hosting a joint event with the debate club on moral considerations in environmental policy.

While finalizing these plans, I smiled at the growth of my network. Our moral inquiry had woven into the fabric of college life, connecting with service, debate, cultural exchange, and personal development. Morality was not confined to a single group; it permeated everything, if only we cared to see it.

On the last day of the semester, I took a solitary walk around campus. The banyan tree stood silent, no discussion session today. Under its branches, scattered leaves reminded me of the many words we shared, the ideas that took root in each participant's mind. I placed my hand on the trunk, grateful for this place that had become a second sanctuary of moral exploration.

Turning away, I spotted a familiar face—one of the students who had attended only one or two sessions. He nodded at me. "Thanks for those discussions," he said softly. "They made me think differently about some choices I've made." I thanked him, touched by the small acknowledgment. This confirmed again that moral influence often goes unseen until someone voices their appreciation.

Walking off the campus, I felt ready for whatever came next. The world beyond the college gates beckoned with infinite moral scenarios. Maybe I'd intern somewhere, facing workplace ethics. Maybe I'd join a civic initiative, applying the lessons of empathy and dialogue on a larger scale. Maybe I'd write about these experiences, inspiring others to reflect on moral action. Regardless of the specific path, I knew I carried the essential tools within me.

Moral courage, I now understood, was not about never feeling fear or confusion. It was about facing them openly. Moral integrity wasn't about perfection, but about striving, learning from mistakes, and listening to others' insights. Empathy wasn't just a feeling—it was a skill, honed by interaction and reflection. Dialogue wasn't just talk—it was a process that revealed shared values, exposed blind spots, and fostered collective growth.

I paused at the bus stop, the city's hum in my ears. I thought of the children's shelter, of Rina's progress in reading, of Jose's apology, of Arjun and Leila's debates, of the reflection wall we once posted notes on. All these moments formed a tapestry of moral learning. Each thread mattered: the old school circle, the college volunteer collective, the banyan tree discussions, and the everyday moral choices I made walking these streets.

Stepping onto the bus, I carried a quiet resolve. Wherever I went, I would continue to seek moral clarity, form communities of dialogue, and act with empathy. I would remain open to critique and new perspectives, recognizing that moral growth never ended. It was a lifelong journey of testing, refining, and expanding one's moral horizon.

As the bus pulled away, I watched the campus recede into the distance. I felt no sadness, just gratitude and anticipation. I had learned that each environment offered a chance to deepen moral understanding, to become more effective in doing good, to inspire others to reflect. The college chapter might close, but the essence of what I cultivated—dialogue, courage, empathy—would guide me into the next chapters of life's moral adventure.

In that gentle motion, I realized fully that I was prepared to face the wider world, a world constantly presenting moral crossroads. And I would not face it alone: I carried within me the voices of those I'd engaged with, the principles we'd tested together, and the memory of transformations achieved through simple acts of communication and kindness.

This realization filled me with a quiet, persistent hope. As long as people were willing to talk, listen, and learn, moral growth was possible. As long as we recognized that no single person had all the answers, but that together we could approach truth asymptotically, we would keep making our communities more humane.

The bus turned a corner, the city's skyline unfolding before me, and I embraced the journey ahead.

V

Consolidating Moral Traditions

9

Weaving Morality into the Tapestry of Daily Life

Years had passed since my college days, and I found myself on the threshold of a new phase—full adulthood, with its tangled responsibilities and freedoms. The idealistic visions I once nurtured under the peepal and banyan trees now had to find footing in a world of offices, bills, neighbors, colleagues, and shifting friendships. The moral insights I'd gained were tools I carried with me, but the landscapes had changed again. Now the challenges were more subtle, woven through professional, social, and civic spheres.

I'd taken a job at a mid-sized social enterprise focused on community development projects. We partnered with local self-help groups, funded small-scale businesses run by women, organized skill-training workshops, and occasionally worked with local government agencies. Our mission statement was simple yet powerful: empower communities through sustainable, participatory approaches. It sounded noble on paper, and I wanted to believe in it fully. Yet I knew from experience that moral complexity lurked behind every kind intention.

The office itself was a modest, two-story building in a busy part of the city. My colleagues ranged from seasoned activists to young professionals fresh out of grad school. Some approached their work with pragmatic realism; others displayed undaunted optimism. A few harbored quiet cynicism, having seen too many projects fail or too many promises broken. As I settled in, I realized I needed to navigate not just the tasks—writing reports, meeting community leaders, evaluating proposals—but the moral undercurrents: how we treated one another internally, how we engaged with the communities we claimed to serve, and how we balanced competing values like efficiency and inclusivity.

In my first weeks, I simply observed. I watched how my supervisor, Raghav, handled conflicting priorities. He was kind and approachable, yet often overworked. I noticed how Anika, one of the senior field officers, treated the villagers with warmth and patience, but sometimes grew frustrated with bureaucratic delays. I saw how a junior employee, Farhan, hesitated to voice his concerns in meetings, fearing rebuke or dismissal.

These dynamics reminded me of earlier lessons: moral reasoning thrived in dialogue, and a healthy environment would welcome diverse voices. But unlike school or college, I wasn't sure how to introduce the idea of moral reflection here without seeming odd or naïve. People were busy, stressed by deadlines, donor expectations, and community demands. Who had time for philosophical chats?

Yet I recognized moral discourse didn't have to be labeled as such. It could emerge organically if I listened and asked thoughtful questions. Over coffee breaks, I struck up conversations. When Farhan complained about never being asked for his input, I empathized, recalling my own early fears of speaking up. "Have you tried sharing your perspective informally with Anika or Raghav?" I suggested. "They might not realize you have valuable insights." He shrugged, uncertain, but I planted a seed.

When Anika lamented that certain community members resisted our interventions, I asked, "Could we find out why they resist? Maybe our approach doesn't align with their priorities." She paused, surprised I was questioning the standard narrative that reluctance meant ignorance. This gentle push encouraged her to consider approaching villagers differently, asking them to shape project goals rather than imposing preconceived plans.

Gradually, I found ways to integrate moral dialogue into the workflow. When we analyzed a new proposal—say, funding a small textile workshop for a women's collective—I'd not only check feasibility and cost but also ask, "How do we ensure this doesn't undercut existing local craftspeople who rely on similar work?" or "How can we guarantee fair wages and respectful treatment of the workers?" These questions made colleagues think more broadly about the ripple effects of our choices.

I also discovered that many colleagues welcomed these discussions once given permission. People often carried moral questions unspoken, afraid to slow down the process. But when someone created a space for it—asking respectfully, acknowledging complexity—they responded. Some admitted it felt refreshing to consider ethical dimensions rather than just technical ones.

Still, this was a workplace, not a reading circle under a tree. We had tangible goals, deadlines, and measurable outcomes to produce. I learned to respect that reality. We couldn't spend hours debating every minor decision. Sometimes we had to move forward with incomplete information. Moral reasoning had to be applied nimbly—brief moments of reflection embedded in decision-making. I learned to be concise: raise a critical question, propose a small adjustment, and then move on. Over time, these small interventions accumulated, influencing the office culture subtly.

Outside of work, my personal life had also expanded. I lived in a small apartment in a mixed neighborhood—young professionals, families, retirees, and recent migrants from rural areas. The building's residents formed a loose community with occasional gatherings: a festival potluck, a cleaning drive, a WhatsApp group to share announcements or ask for help. Navigating this environment tested my moral compass in new, everyday ways. When a neighbor's child cried late at night, disturbing my sleep, I had to choose empathy over irritation—knowing they might be struggling with a sick baby. When the building's maintenance funds were mismanaged by a resident committee member, I had to speak up diplomatically, encouraging transparency without causing antagonism.

One incident stands out: a conflict arose when a few residents wanted to exclude a family newly arrived from another region, complaining that their cooking smells and language were "too different." Old biases surfaced, reminiscent of the stereotypes I'd confronted in school and college discussions. This time, I felt a responsibility to intervene—not as an outsider, but as a member of this community.

I approached a neighbor who seemed sympathetic and suggested we organize a small, informal "cultural evening" where families could share stories, recipes, or music from their backgrounds. The idea was to celebrate diversity rather than tolerate it grudgingly. Some balked at first, but a handful agreed to help. On the chosen evening, people gathered hesitantly in the building's communal area. The new family brought a traditional snack; others brought different treats. Initially stiff, the atmosphere softened as people tasted each other's foods and listened to short anecdotes. The previously maligned cooking smells were now intriguing flavors to explore.

This simple gathering didn't erase all prejudices overnight, but it opened a door. Over time, neighbors became friendlier, acknowledging each other in hallways and even asking for recipes. I saw again how moral action often involved subtle interventions—finding common ground, humanizing the "other," creating platforms for empathy.

At times, I yearned for the structured moral dialogues of my past—those safe, intentional sessions under the trees where everyone knew we were there to reflect deeply. Now moral inquiries were scattered across professional meetings, hallway chats, neighborhood discussions, family conversations. Yet this dispersion was also a sign of growth: my moral practice had matured to the point where I could integrate it into ordinary life without special frameworks or formal events. Morality had become an ongoing, quiet dimension of my relationships and choices.

Another challenging scenario emerged at work when we partnered with a local government office to implement a training program for unemployed youth. Funding was limited, and the government official overseeing the grant implied that if we "streamlined" certain paperwork or overlooked some irregularities, things would move faster. This was a moral test: do we compromise integrity for expediency, justifying it by the project's noble goal (providing job skills to youth)?

I discussed the issue with Raghav and Anika. They were torn—delay could jeopardize the entire project, denying hundreds of young people opportunities. But what precedent would we set by bending rules? And who would be hurt if we established a relationship based on partial dishonesty?

Recalling my earlier lessons, I suggested approaching the official again, but this time asking specific questions: Which documents does he consider unnecessary and why? Could we simplify compliance without violating core principles? Perhaps we could find a middle path—improving efficiency while maintaining transparency. We drafted a letter detailing which steps we were willing to revise for clarity but insisting on proper accountability measures. This firm yet flexible stance communicated that we cared about both effectiveness and ethics.

The official, initially expecting easy compliance, hesitated. But when he realized we wouldn't yield on integrity, he decided to cooperate within legal bounds rather than lose the partnership. It wasn't a grand triumph of morality over corruption—perhaps he was just pragmatically adjusting—but it demonstrated that moral firmness, combined with open dialogue, could influence outcomes.

In my personal sphere, I also navigated moral questions. I started a relationship with someone I met through the service network. We shared values but had different temperaments. Conflict arose when discussing career plans—my partner felt I sometimes prioritized work over quality time. Did I owe it to them and our relationship to adjust my schedule, or was my work equally important? Moral reasoning guided me to consider fairness, communication, and empathy. We found compromises: setting aside regular evenings to be together, and I more consciously balanced my obligations. This reminded me that morality wasn't just about big social issues—it touched intimate, personal decisions too. Being kind, honest, and considerate to a loved one tested my moral integrity as much as any public action.

Sometimes, nostalgia for the old reading circles still tugged at me. I missed the simplicity of those gatherings, where moral dialogue was the explicit purpose. In the adult world, moral conversations often emerged unpredictably and ended abruptly, overshadowed by deadlines or distractions. Yet I understood that this was the ultimate moral test: applying lessons spontaneously, without a curated environment. Life wouldn't always give me perfect conditions for reflection; I had to carve out reflective moments on my own.

When I yearned for deeper discussion, I'd invite a few friends from work or neighbors I trusted for a casual dinner. Over a meal, we'd slip into conversations about the projects we handled, the biases we encountered, or the hopes we had for positive change. We never officially called it a "moral dialogue group," but it served a similar function—exchanging perspectives, challenging assumptions, reinforcing shared values. These informal circles became my adult version of the banyan tree sessions, dispersed across multiple evenings, different guests, and shifting topics.

Over the years, I noticed subtle but meaningful shifts in my environment. At the office, others began asking moral questions without prompting: "Before we finalize this proposal, should we consider the local artisans who might be affected?" In the neighborhood, new families were welcomed more openly, as people remembered the cultural evening that had broken down initial barriers. Farhan, the once timid junior employee, became more assertive in expressing his insights, having learned from our early coffee-break chats that his voice mattered.

I also faced failures. Some communities we tried to help rejected our initiatives altogether, feeling patronized. I had to accept that moral intentions didn't guarantee welcome. In those cases, the moral response was humility—revisiting assumptions, listening more closely, maybe stepping back to let the community lead. Morality required resilience: not giving up on principles after a setback, but recalibrating strategies.

Over time, I came to see morality as a tapestry we weave daily with countless threads: words chosen in a difficult conversation, decisions made in a rushed meeting, kindness extended to a stranger, accountability demanded from a partner. Each action, however small, added color and pattern to the whole. The tapestry was never complete; each day brought new threads to weave.

Sometimes I wondered what the younger me—standing silently in a school corridor, terrified to speak—would think if they saw me now. I hoped they'd be proud: I had taken that initial fear and transformed it into an ongoing moral practice. Fear had not vanished, but it no longer paralyzed me. It had become a guide, indicating where courage and reflection were needed.

In moments of doubt, I revisited old notes and reflections I'd written over the years. Skimming through them, I saw continuity: the early discovery that dialogue fosters moral growth in school; the college sessions under the banyan tree linking personal choices to systemic issues; and now this adult life, embedding moral awareness into professional and community settings. The essence remained: morality thrives in relationships, complexity is inevitable, and the best we can do is stay open, curious, and empathetic.

As new opportunities arose—perhaps I'd lead a new project or mediate a dispute between colleagues—I continued to rely on these moral muscles. I asked myself: What values are at stake here? Whose voices need hearing? How can we act with integrity without falling into rigidity? The answers varied, but the process was consistent: reflection, consultation, and a willingness to adapt.

One day, Anika approached me after a tough field visit. "I've been doing this work for years," she said, looking tired. "Sometimes I lose faith. We try so hard, yet we face corruption, apathy, or cultural obstacles. How do we keep going without despairing?"

I thought back to the many times I'd felt similar discouragement. "It helps to remember that moral growth is incremental," I replied. "We may not transform whole systems overnight, but each sincere effort, each respectful conversation, plants seeds. We build trust, foster empathy, and maybe inspire others to reflect. Over time, these small changes accumulate."

She nodded slowly. "So you're saying it's about patience and faith in the process?"

"Exactly," I said. "We can't control everything, but we can influence our immediate circles. Our actions ripple out in ways we might never fully see."

Her shoulders relaxed slightly, comforted. I realized that providing moral encouragement was itself a moral act—supporting colleagues, nurturing their resilience and hope. Morality wasn't just about criticizing wrongdoing or making tough decisions; it was also about uplifting each other in the face of complexity.

Months later, I had a chance to organize a workshop for new

employees. Instead of focusing solely on technical training, I added a small session about "Ethical Engagement with Communities." I invited a respected community leader to speak, someone who had experienced both well-intentioned interventions that fell flat and those that truly empowered locals. Listening to her stories, the newcomers saw how moral considerations shaped trust and long-term impact. We discussed how to ask communities what they needed rather than dictating solutions, how to share credit rather than claiming heroism, and how to maintain honesty even when pressured to show quick results.

This workshop felt like a full-circle moment: I was formally integrating moral dialogue into professional development. The participants responded well, raising their own moral dilemmas and brainstorming solutions. It wasn't a magic fix, but it signaled that morality could be part of institutional culture if nurtured.

Outside of work, I continued engaging with my neighborhood. Over time, we formed a small residents' committee dedicated to inclusive activities—regular cultural nights, skill-sharing sessions, and addressing conflicts through mediation rather than hostility. When disputes arose (like noise complaints or misunderstandings about shared spaces), we approached them collectively, inviting all parties to explain their perspectives. This mirrored the early reading circles, but now in a messy, real-world context where people had competing interests and histories.

Through these efforts, I learned that moral living doesn't always produce dramatic outcomes. Often it's quieter: reduced tension, a neighbor smiling instead of scowling, a coworker pausing to reconsider a decision. Yet these quiet shifts matter. They create an environment where more thoughtful actions become possible. Over time, moral habits can accumulate into a community that handles differences more gracefully, a workplace that respects dignity, and individuals who approach life's puzzles with greater integrity.

As the years went by, I embraced that I was not the same person who needed structured circles to talk about ethics. Now I could spontaneously weave moral reflection into everyday life. Yet I also realized the value of occasionally stepping back and reconnecting with that structured reflection when possible—hosting a small dinner for friends to discuss a challenging social issue or inviting colleagues to reflect on lessons learned from a failed project. These moments re-energized my moral perspective and reminded me that while morality must be flexible and integrated, intentional reflection remains crucial.

I also recognized that moral growth requires continuous learning. I read widely: articles on ethical leadership, accounts of humanitarian efforts gone awry, stories of local heroes making small differences. I attended a workshop on conflict resolution techniques. I spoke with mentors and younger colleagues alike, learning from their experiences. Moral understanding, I found, expands when we treat life as a classroom without walls.

In these ways, the moral lessons I gained in youth matured into a lifelong practice. The essence was always the same: respect complexity, listen deeply, dialogue openly, act with empathy, remain humble before uncertainty, and never stop learning. Morality, I discovered, is not a destination or a badge of honor—it's a discipline of navigating life's evolving tapestry, thread by careful thread.

Looking back, I realized that my journey had formed a coherent narrative after all. The initial fear and silence in school sparked a quest for moral voice and community; college broadened my horizons, showing systemic dimensions; adulthood challenged me to integrate moral reasoning into practical action. Each stage refined my moral faculties, teaching me that nothing is static—human understanding, societies, and personal roles keep changing. Moral growth, therefore, is about adapting principles to new conditions without losing sight of core values.

As I approached another stage—perhaps taking on more leadership at work, considering a family of my own, or moving to a new city—I knew moral dilemmas would follow me. Perhaps I'd face ethical trade-offs in resource allocation for larger projects, or help children I might one day raise understand kindness and justice, or join community movements tackling environmental crises. For each new challenge, I would rely on the practice I'd honed: moral inquiry as a lifelong companion.

In quiet moments, I sometimes closed my eyes and imagined sitting again under the peepal tree at my old school, or the banyan tree at college, or the small gatherings in my apartment or office. I imagined all those who'd joined me in discussions over the years—the classmates, peers, neighbors, colleagues, and mentors—sitting together in a vast, timeless circle. Even those who were no longer present in my life contributed to the tapestry of my moral understanding. Their voices lived on in my memory, guiding me gently.

This sense of collective moral learning gave me faith. Despite the world's cruelty and complexity, despite personal failures and systemic injustices, we had tools: conversation, empathy, self-awareness, creativity. Applying them required courage, patience, and perseverance, but it was always worth trying. Each moral effort, however modest, helped prevent despair and cynicism from taking root.

So, standing at another crossroad in life, I felt prepared to face what lay ahead. The moral tapestry I'd woven was strong enough to endure new strains and flexible enough to adapt to new patterns. I carried forward the lessons of my past—no longer confined to youthful idealism, but grounded in mature understanding. My voice, once trembling, was steady. My empathy, once hesitant, was confident. My openness to complexity, once fragile, was now resilient.

In this realization, I found a quiet peace: that moral growth, nurtured through dialogues and actions over a lifetime, could make daily life richer, more meaningful, and more humane. Nothing guaranteed easy solutions, but at least I knew how to ask better questions, how to listen more deeply, and how to act with integrity even when no one was watching.

With that peace settled in my heart, I stepped forward into the day—an adult fully engaged in the world's moral struggles, guided by a lifetime of practice and the knowledge that this practice would never end, only deepen.

10

Passing the Torch of Moral Reasoning

A hush settled over the city one afternoon, an unusual stillness that felt like the air itself was holding its breath. I leaned against my office window—now on a higher floor than years before, reflecting a slow rise in my responsibilities—and watched dust motes swirl in the sunlight. Decades had passed since I first stood silently in a school corridor, unsure how to raise my voice. Now, strands of gray touched my hair, and lines of experience etched the corners of my eyes. The moral tapestry I'd woven through countless interactions had grown dense and intricate. Yet, as life often does, it was about to present me with a fresh moral crucible.

In recent years, I had taken on a leadership role within the social enterprise where I worked. The organization had expanded its scope: we now partnered not only with local communities but also with regional networks, coordinating with environmental groups, civic associations, and policy advocates. Our projects had grown more ambitious, tackling resource allocation, social inequality, and climate resilience. This complexity demanded moral reasoning on a grander scale, testing whether the principles I'd cherished could withstand political pressures, competing interests, and high-stakes decisions affecting thousands of lives.

A looming crisis had been brewing for weeks. A severe drought affected the entire region. Crops failed, rivers shrank, and communities that once thrived on small-scale agriculture hovered on the brink of scarcity. The government's initial response floundered—slow bureaucracy, outdated water management policies, and miscommunication abounded. Tensions rose as different groups fought over limited water resources. Some advocated diverting water from one set of fields to another. Others demanded immediate restrictions on urban consumption. Environmental activists warned that hasty interventions might cause long-term ecological damage.

Our organization found itself at the center of these debates, asked to mediate because we had earned a reputation for balanced moral reasoning. We were neither a pure advocacy group nor a government entity; we straddled a line of trust. Over the years, through quiet moral inquiries and earnest dialogue, we had built credibility. Now everyone wanted a piece of that credibility—farmers hoping for their survival, urban planners seeking stability, environmentalists protecting ecosystems, and officials praying for a solution that wouldn't spark unrest.

As I listened to proposals from all sides, I felt the gravity of the moment. This was no simple matter of helping children read or discussing everyday ethics under a banyan tree. Lives and livelihoods depended on the choices we made. My own moral compass, honed through personal relationships and community-level projects, now had to guide decisions on a scale I'd never faced. Yet the principles remained the same: respect complexity, seek dialogue, uphold empathy, find solutions that honor human dignity and ecological integrity.

I convened a series of dialogues modeled after the smaller moral circles I had experienced throughout my life. But this time, we gathered in a large community hall near a dried-up riverbed—symbolic of the crisis at hand. Representatives came from various factions: local farmers whose fields lay cracked and barren, city officials worried about drinking water supplies, environmental scientists warning of long-term collapse if we mismanaged this moment, and activists who insisted on equitable distribution to marginalized communities. Dozens of people, each with their own interests, their own fears.

My stomach knotted as I stood before them. Once, I had quaked just asking a question in class. Now I faced a room of anxious, frustrated people, some suspicious, some desperate. But I remembered the lessons: courage coexists with fear, dialogue thrives despite tension, and acknowledging uncertainty can build trust. I introduced the session as an attempt not to impose solutions but to discover common ground.

"We're here to understand each other's perspectives," I said, voice steady but warm. "We know water is scarce. We know everyone's survival is at stake. Let's start by identifying core values. What do we all cherish?"

At first, responses were guarded. The farmers muttered that they cherished their families and their right to work the land. Urban planners emphasized societal stability and economic continuity. Environmentalists stressed biodiversity and future generations' wellbeing. On the surface, these sounded conflicting. But as I guided the conversation, I asked: "Don't we all care about life, fairness, and hope for the future?"

Heads nodded reluctantly. Even those entrenched in their positions admitted that they didn't wish harm on others. This initial admission of common humanity, small yet crucial, resembled the early steps of moral dialogues I'd held in simpler contexts. Even at this large scale, people responded to empathy and careful listening.

Over multiple sessions, we dissected options: rationing schemes, reforestation to increase water retention, temporary transfers of water rights from less-affected areas, investment in rainwater harvesting infrastructure. Each proposal carried moral costs and benefits. Would diverting water to save some farms cause others to fail? Would prioritizing urban drinking water mean rural families starved? We confronted these dilemmas openly, acknowledging that no choice was perfect.

My role was not to dictate solutions but to maintain a moral framework. When a faction grew hostile—farmers accusing city dwellers of greed—I asked them to consider that city families included poor laborers who couldn't afford skyrocketing food prices if agriculture collapsed. When city officials demanded priority, I reminded them that rural communities had historically borne burdens for urban growth, and justice required compensating for past imbalances. For environmentalists pushing for strict ecological limits, I asked how we could also ensure human survival as we transitioned to sustainable practices.

This balancing act resembled the moral tightrope I'd walked many times before, but now magnified. I drew on everything I'd learned: how small acts of empathy eased tensions, how acknowledging uncertainty fostered humility, how inviting everyone to shape the process prevented one group from feeling overrun. These were the same principles that had guided me in a classroom debate, a college volunteer project, or a workplace dispute—but now applied to a regional crisis.

Progress was incremental. No one left these meetings wholly satisfied. Yet after weeks of persistent dialogue, we reached a set of provisional agreements: a tiered rationing system that prioritized drinking water and essential crops, coupled with swift investment in rainwater harvesting and infrastructural projects to build long-term resilience. The environmentalists agreed to these measures because we included timelines and binding commitments for ecological restoration. The farmers accepted certain restrictions because we guaranteed technical support to transition to drought-resistant crops.

The city officials yielded some immediate privileges in exchange for community cooperation and stability.

It felt like a fragile mosaic, held together by mutual compromise and moral goodwill. I knew it might crack under pressure if conditions worsened. But it was a moral beginning, a roadmap created not by force or trickery but by moral discourse, empathy, and an understanding of complexity. As we concluded the final meeting, people shook hands warily. Some even managed a half-smile. I glimpsed the power of sustained moral reasoning to guide collective decision-making, just as it had guided personal choices earlier in my life.

In the aftermath of these negotiations, I felt both relief and exhaustion. The agreement wasn't a panacea—drought and climate instability demanded ongoing effort. But we had prevented immediate chaos and laid a foundation for more ethical governance of scarce resources. As I returned to my office, I reflected on how far I'd come. The moral reasoning once practiced in safe, small circles now shaped a region's fate. This was the ultimate validation of the principles I'd held dear: dialogue, empathy, and respect for complexity truly could scale.

Outside of work, my personal life had also evolved. My partner and I had formed a family—two children now scampered through our home, their laughter and questions infusing life with new moral dimensions. Guiding children introduced another layer of moral responsibility. They asked questions: Why do some people struggle to find clean water? Why must we share toys or help neighbors? I recognized these as openings to pass on moral habits—listening, empathy, questioning assumptions. I told them stories of my younger self: how I learned to overcome fear, how moral conversations helped me understand right and wrong more fully. I encouraged them to ask their own questions, form their own moral circles with friends, and not fear uncertainty.

I saw the cycle repeating: just as I once learned from elders, mentors, and peers, now I was a mentor. My children's eyes widened when I described how people from different backgrounds learned to talk and compromise over something as essential as water. They marveled that adults listened to each other instead of fighting. Perhaps these seeds of moral reasoning would bloom in them, guiding their future challenges.

Beyond family, I also mentored younger colleagues at work. Some struggled with the moral complexities of development projects. They asked me how to handle conflicts between community wishes and donor expectations. I encouraged them to create spaces for moral dialogue within project teams, to invite community members to co-design solutions, and to remain humble before complexity. Transmitting these lessons filled me with quiet satisfaction, ensuring that moral reasoning lived not just in my actions but in those I influenced.

At times, I reconnected with old friends—Arjun, Leila, and Jose from college, or Sahana and Dev from my earlier career days. We reflected on how the moral seeds we planted long ago had grown into widespread branches of influence. Arjun, involved in policy advocacy, told me that remembering our banyan tree discussions helped him remain honest even when lobbyists pressured him. Leila, now a psychologist working with marginalized communities, said our old debates about empathy shaped her counseling methods. Jose, who once apologized after a careless joke, had become known in his own circle for encouraging respectful communication. We realized that moral reasoning had rippled through our social networks, changing not just us but those we touched.

In the neighborhood, I continued to foster inclusive traditions. When new families arrived—migrants, refugees, or just people from distant parts of the country—we held gatherings to learn about their cuisines, music, and stories. By now, this was an established ritual, expected and welcomed. Moral openness had become part of the neighborhood's cultural fabric. Conflicts still arose, but we handled them with slightly more grace, remembering that listening and understanding often defused tensions better than shouting.

Occasionally, I faced new moral dilemmas that challenged my evolved perspective. One instance involved a technological initiative: a partner organization proposed using digital tools to track community resource usage. They argued it would improve efficiency, but I worried about privacy and data misuse. Was efficiency worth risking people's autonomy and dignity? I convened a small moral circle within my team—an echo of old habits—asking each person to voice concerns. By weighing efficiency against privacy, we concluded that we must include strict data protection measures and informed consent protocols. Thus, moral reasoning shaped our embrace of technology, ensuring progress didn't erode human values.

As I grew older, I understood that moral reasoning never promised an end to difficulties. On the contrary, life remained complex, often presenting moral puzzles without easy solutions. But I no longer found that discouraging. Instead, it confirmed that morality was a living, adaptive practice. Just as muscles stay strong through regular exercise, moral clarity emerged from continuous engagement with tough questions. The world changed; I changed; our moral tapestry evolved with new patterns, new colors, new knots to untangle.

Reflecting on my journey, I saw that I'd created a legacy. Not a formal institution or a grand philosophical treatise, but a legacy of practice. My actions, dialogues, and mentorship had sown moral inquiry in many places and people. The seeds I once planted in school and college had borne fruit in workplaces, communities, crisis negotiations, and family life. Countless individuals now carried forward the spirit of moral dialogue: younger colleagues who facilitated respectful debate in their teams, neighbors who welcomed diversity rather than fearing it, children who learned to ask "Why?" and "Who is affected?" before judging.

This realization filled me with hope. The world's challenges were immense—climate change, political polarization, economic injustice—but the tools of moral reasoning scaled as well. If one person could influence a handful, who in turn influenced others, then moral inquiry could spread like roots beneath the surface, stabilizing the social soil. True, we lacked tidy conclusions or universal consensus, but maybe moral growth didn't require perfect consensus—just better processes for handling disagreements, more empathy in negotiations, and a willingness to revisit assumptions.

Now advanced in my career and life, I looked beyond immediate tasks. I imagined starting a multi-generational moral forum, inviting elders and youth to share perspectives. Could we create a space where retirees reflected on past moral lessons and students proposed innovative ethical frameworks for the future? Intergenerational dialogue appealed to me, bridging past wisdom and youthful insight. Perhaps I'd organize such a forum in the community hall where we once negotiated the drought crisis, symbolically returning to that place of moral convergence.

As the idea formed in my mind, I realized how natural it felt to initiate these moral platforms. Once, I needed courage to speak in small groups. Now I instinctively created larger arenas for moral conversation. The arc of my moral journey was clear: from fearful silence to confident facilitation, from personal growth to communal guidance, from local interventions to regional crisis management, and now toward ensuring moral reflection passed seamlessly to future generations.

One weekend, I invited my children—now teenagers—and a group of their friends to a casual discussion at home. I set out snacks and juice, and asked if they wanted to talk about anything troubling or confusing them. At first, they teased me: "Dad, are we having one of your 'philosophy chats' again?" I laughed but persisted. Eventually, they brought up issues from their school: bullying, pressure to conform, online rumors that spread cruelty with a click. These were moral dilemmas of their era, filtered through social media and fast-changing norms.

I listened as they expressed frustration and uncertainty. Then I nudged them gently. "What if you approached these problems as moral puzzles, not just annoyances? Can you try understanding why a bully behaves that way, or how a rumor starts and spreads? Maybe you can form a small group to discuss respectful online behavior, just like I did with my friends long ago."

They rolled their eyes slightly—teenagers testing boundaries—but a spark lit in some of their expressions. The seed was planted, as others had been planted in me. In time, they might form their own moral circles, adapting our old methods to new technologies and contexts. I felt reassured that moral reasoning would endure beyond my active influence, carried by younger voices into an unknown future.

As I approached another transition—perhaps retirement or shifting into a more advisory role—I reflected on the tapestry woven from my life's moral threads. Each chapter had introduced new settings and challenges. Each time, the principles held: dialogue, empathy, integrity, humility. Across decades, I never discovered a final, fixed moral formula. Instead, I learned that morality was an art, and I had become an artist skilled at blending colors of compassion and lines of fairness, shading complexities and highlighting values.

In a final act of synthesis, I decided to write an informal guide: not a rigid manual, but a reflective essay documenting key lessons from my lifelong moral practice. I'd call it something like "Threads of Dialogue: A Life in Moral Reasoning." In it, I described the early fear and silence, the school sessions, the college reading group, the workplace initiatives, the community engagements, and the large-scale negotiations. I emphasized that anyone, anywhere, could start moral conversations—no special authority or expertise required. Just curiosity, respect, and courage.

I kept the tone humble, acknowledging my mistakes and uncertainties. I recounted how no solution was perfect, how sometimes I failed or backtracked, but each effort taught me something. I included anecdotes where moral inquiry saved relationships, prevented conflicts, and inspired creative solutions. I hoped this essay, shared informally with colleagues, neighbors, and family, might encourage others to weave their own moral tapestries. Maybe it would circulate beyond my immediate circle—who knew?

As I wrote, I recognized that my life's moral journey had never been solitary. It had always been collaborative, shaped by others' contributions and receptiveness. I hoped that by documenting my story, I would honor all those who engaged in moral dialogue with me—the teachers, classmates, peers, mentors, family members, colleagues, neighbors, and community members. Their voices had blended with mine, co-creating a moral language that transcended any individual.

On a crisp morning, I printed the essay and handed copies to a few trusted friends and colleagues. Some thanked me, others promised to read and share it. My children smirked at the old-fashioned paper copies but stored a digital version. I knew moral insights had to adapt to new forms—digital forums, podcasts, social media groups—just as I once adapted to adult responsibilities and large-scale issues. Let others reinterpret and innovate.

A few weeks later, a younger colleague approached me, essay in hand, eyes shining. She said it helped her understand how to handle a delicate situation with a local women's cooperative. They felt overshadowed by more outspoken groups, and she now planned to hold a moral inquiry session inviting them to shape the project goals. This direct, immediate feedback reassured me that the chain continued: my reflections now fueled new moral endeavors led by another generation.

In my mind's eye, I pictured a vast tapestry stretching across time and space. My threads were woven alongside countless others—those who had inspired me and those I inspired in turn. The tapestry showed no clear pattern at first glance, but if one looked closely, they'd see themes emerging: compassion woven into justice, honesty twined with courage, humility interlaced with perseverance. The tapestry kept growing as more people learned to add their moral threads, strengthening and diversifying the weave.

In this vision, moral reasoning was never static. It flowed through dialogues, bore fruit in relationships and decisions, adapted to crises, and passed along to future hands. I had played my part: from timid silence to confident guidance, from seeking understanding to helping others seek theirs. Now, as life moved me toward more reflective years, I trusted that moral inquiry would outlast me, continuing to shape communities, families, workplaces, and souls I would never meet.

I contemplated the future challenges my children and their peers would face—accelerating technology, climate upheavals, shifting cultural landscapes. They would need moral reasoning more than ever. But now, they had something to guide them: a tradition, even if informal, of dialogue and empathy. They might refine or reinvent these practices, just as I had adapted them to new environments. The core principle would remain: morality emerges through honest engagement with complexity.

As the sun lowered on another day, I stepped outside for a walk. The air felt lighter, as if the city breathed easier after the drought crisis had stabilized. People milled about in the streets, each with their own moral stories unfolding privately. I imagined countless moral inquiries happening quietly—a friend advising another to apologize, a parent teaching a child to share, a manager incorporating fairness into a new policy. Most of these acts would go unnoticed, uncelebrated, yet each strand contributed to a more humane world.

Strolling through a park, I passed a group of teenagers huddled over their phones. Perhaps they debated online ethics or climate responsibility. Nearby, an older couple assisted a stranger carrying heavy bags—a small moral deed unremarkable yet significant. A community garden displayed a sign asking visitors to take only what they needed and leave produce for others—someone's moral reasoning had shaped this note, trusting in people's capacity for fairness.

These everyday scenes were the legacy of moral inquiry: it taught us to care about others' perspectives, to anticipate consequences, to imagine better outcomes, and to anchor our lives in shared values. Not everyone practiced it consciously, but the more people who learned these habits, the more they influenced the culture, nudging it toward empathy, justice, and collaboration.

Returning home, I felt calm and resolved. My journey didn't end with chapter 10—life would continue testing my moral mettle. But I accepted that no final chapter existed. Moral growth lasted a lifetime, and when my time passed, others would write their own chapters, guided partly by the work I had done and the values I had shared.

Stepping through my front door, I heard the familiar laughter of my children and partner, felt the warmth of a place shaped by mutual respect and love. I knew that tomorrow or next week, some moral question would arise—a disagreement over chores, a neighbor's complaint, a work dilemma—and I would once again apply the same approach: listen, reflect, empathize, negotiate, learn.

This constancy reassured me. Morality was not a burden, but a sustaining force that made life meaningful. Each moral decision reinforced the tapestry, adding texture and dimension. Even when mistakes occurred, we learned and grew wiser. Over years and generations, this collective learning slowly improved how we lived together on this fragile planet.

As the night deepened, I allowed myself one last reflection. From frightened silence in a school corridor to facilitating regional negotiations, from intimate conversations to public dialogues, I had proven that moral reasoning could be cultivated anywhere. Morality wasn't the domain of philosophers alone; it belonged to all who dared to engage with others and face complexity.

I closed my eyes, picturing the future. Perhaps my children would form their own moral circles with friends, tackling issues I couldn't imagine—artificial intelligence ethics, new resource conflicts, cultural shifts unimaginable today. They would find their way, using the same tools: dialogue, empathy, humility, a willingness to listen and adapt. And so the tapestry would grow ever richer, ensuring that moral inquiry remained a living tradition, passed hand to hand, heart to heart.

With a gentle smile, I stepped into the next day, confident that although the world remained imperfect and uncertain, the practice of moral reasoning I helped nurture would continue guiding many souls toward understanding, kindness, and hope.

VI

Ensuring the Practice Endures

11

A Legacy of Moral Inquiry

In the quiet predawn, I rose from bed slowly, bones protesting with age. The air in my room was still, and outside the window, the city I'd known for so long lay half-asleep, silhouettes of buildings under a faint glow. Decades had slipped by since I first learned to raise my voice in moral conversation. Now, silver streaked my hair freely, and my joints ached. My children were grown, carving out their own paths in a world that felt simultaneously familiar and strange. My partner and I had settled into a rhythm of gentle days, punctuated by the occasional excitement of visits from grandchildren or the arrival of a new project at the social enterprise I'd helped guide.

Yet as I dressed that morning, I sensed unrest in the world around me. The city had changed again—more crowded, more digitally connected, yet also facing sharper divides. Climate events now arrived with alarming frequency: floods in seasons that should be dry, droughts when we needed rain. Economic strains had deepened old inequalities. Political rhetoric in recent years had grown more polarized, less willing to acknowledge moral complexity. All this weighed on my heart. Was the moral tapestry we'd woven over generations fraying under pressure?

I made my way to a modest community center we had established a few years back. We called it the "Moral Inquiry Forum," a dedicated space where people could come to discuss ethical challenges facing the city and region. It was my attempt to institutionalize what I'd practiced informally throughout life: a place for structured, inclusive, empathy-driven conversations about how to live together ethically. We held regular sessions, welcomed diverse voices, and sometimes hosted intergenerational gatherings. My hope was that, long after I was gone, the forum would keep moral reasoning alive as a community tradition.

Today, however, the forum faced a formidable test. News had spread of a looming political crisis: a proposed government policy threatened to displace entire neighborhoods to make way for a large-scale infrastructure project—an elevated highway designed to connect affluent city centers with emerging business zones. Proponents argued it would boost economic growth. Opponents warned it would destroy historic communities, uproot thousands of residents, and funnel resources away from pressing environmental restorations.

Tensions soared. Protests formed on the streets. Some demanded outright resistance, others urged negotiation. The policy's defenders accused critics of holding back progress. Many feared violence if the government pushed forward without compromise. The Moral Inquiry Forum had been asked—unofficially—to host a series of emergency dialogues, hoping to find some moral consensus or at least reduce the chance of unrest.

As I entered the building that morning, I found a circle of chairs arranged in the central hall. Volunteers had prepared tea and simple refreshments. On a side table, I saw a printout of guiding principles we'd developed: "Listen before judging. Seek human stories. Embrace complexity. Aim for solutions that honor dignity and fairness." Reading these words, I recalled my earliest steps into moral reasoning, how far I'd traveled. Now, these principles would guide not just me but a large, diverse gathering.

Representatives would arrive soon—community elders from threatened neighborhoods, young entrepreneurs who saw opportunities in the project, environmental groups alarmed by potential ecological damage, and government aides willing to discuss adjustments. This wouldn't be easy. Each faction came entrenched in their views, tired of broken promises and half-truths. Yet I trusted that moral reasoning, honestly applied, could at least open a channel of understanding.

Within an hour, people trickled in. Tension stiffened the air. I greeted them warmly, introducing myself not as an authority but as a facilitator. I explained that the forum existed for moral inquiry, not to impose solutions. "We're here because we care about this city's future," I said softly. "Each of you brings concerns that matter. Let's find a way to acknowledge them and seek common moral ground, even if we can't find perfect agreement."

At first, voices were raised, accusations flew. One side accused the government of catering to elites, another group argued that without infrastructure upgrades, the economy would stagnate, causing future suffering. Environmentalists warned that reckless construction would worsen floods and heatwaves. Residents from threatened areas lamented the potential loss of homes, cultural heritage, and community bonds. I let them vent, understanding that moral discourse sometimes begins with releasing frustration.

After the initial storm, I gently intervened: "Let's step back. Beyond our differences, what values do we share?" A silence followed. I prompted further: "Do we agree that any solution should strive to preserve human dignity, protect the vulnerable, and ensure future generations aren't saddled with irreversible harm?"

Heads nodded reluctantly. Even the fiercest proponents of the highway conceded that no one wanted mass suffering. The environmentalists acknowledged the importance of stable livelihoods. The community elders admitted some infrastructure improvements were needed, if done ethically. Slowly, by naming shared values, we created a moral baseline—a starting point.

The next hours resembled an advanced form of the moral dialogues I'd conducted throughout life, except now the stakes were colossal. I encouraged each side to tell personal stories: a grandmother spoke of her family's generational roots in the neighborhood, a young entrepreneur explained her dream of efficient transport unlocking opportunities for thousands of job-seekers, an environmental scientist described witnessing species decline due to unchecked development. By personalizing their perspectives, we humanized each other, preventing the debate from collapsing into slogans.

Some participants questioned this slow approach. "We need action, not just talk," someone said. But I held firm: "Moral clarity emerges from understanding. Action without understanding risks injustice." Gradually, they saw the value in taking time to listen, to consider moral implications rather than rushing to impose decisions.

As the day wore on, we brainstormed alternatives: Could the highway's route be adjusted to spare vital cultural sites and minimize displacement? Could we invest in relocation assistance that truly respected community ties, not just offering token compensation but ensuring social fabrics remained intact? Could environmental safeguards be mandated, integrating green corridors and flood mitigation measures into the project design?

No one found a perfect solution. Compromise often felt painful. But unlike polarized shouting matches outside, here we explored modifications that balanced different moral goods: economic growth tempered by social justice and ecological responsibility. Representatives from the government took notes, intrigued by the forum's calm atmosphere. Perhaps, I thought, they realized moral reasoning could guide policy better than brute political bargaining.

Yet my realism told me we wouldn't solve everything in one session. I stressed that moral inquiry is iterative. "We've formed initial proposals," I said toward evening, "but we must continue refining them. This is the first step: acknowledging complexity and forging moral principles to guide negotiations." Tired yet somewhat hopeful, participants agreed to reconvene.

As they departed, a government aide pulled me aside. "I never thought we could have such a civil conversation," she admitted. "Usually, I deal with protests or closed-door deals. This forum showed that people can reason together if given the right environment."

I nodded, feeling both pride and responsibility. The Moral Inquiry Forum had proven its worth as a moral infrastructure—a place where moral threads could be woven into public decision-making. Still, I knew the hard work lay ahead: turning these dialogues into concrete policies. But I trusted that with ongoing moral discourse, solutions could evolve.

After everyone left, I lingered, reflecting on my life's arc. Here I stood, late in life, helping guide a large-scale moral conversation. Each stage of my journey had prepared me: the timid beginnings in school taught me courage, college discussions expanded my worldview, workplace dialogues refined my practice, community engagements gave me confidence, and now, well into my elder years, I drew on all that experience to navigate moral crises no one individual could solve alone.

My grandchildren's faces sprang to mind. They were teenagers now, grappling with their own moral questions—online bullying, climate anxiety, cultural tensions in their schools. I decided it was time to invite them into these broader dialogues, to let them see moral reasoning at work beyond home conversations. Maybe I'd bring them to the next forum session, not as participants forced to care but as observers who could learn how grown-ups handle complexity.

The following week, I spoke with my children, explaining the importance of exposing their kids to these moral processes. They agreed, and one bright morning, my grandchildren stood by my side as a follow-up session began. Wide-eyed, they watched adults from different backgrounds attempt to refine the earlier proposals. They listened to stories of displacement and ecological fragility, of economic dreams and cultural traditions.

During a break, one grandchild whispered, "Grandpa, it's so complicated. How do you know who's right?" I smiled gently. "We rarely find a single 'right' answer. We look for ways to reduce harm, respect people's dignity, and care for the future. It's like solving a puzzle where all pieces matter."

They nodded, not fully understanding but intrigued. I realized that by witnessing this moral discourse, they might internalize the idea that complexity isn't scary—it's a natural part of ethical living. If fear and confusion prevented me from speaking in my youth, now I showed them that we can face confusion together, forging understanding through dialogue.

In subsequent meetings, the forum honed the tentative compromises into more detailed plans. An interdisciplinary committee formed, blending community representatives, planners, and environmental experts. They agreed on principles: no relocation without robust community input, mandatory green infrastructure elements to offset environmental impacts, and phased implementation so that communities could adapt gradually. The government officials found the moral arguments persuasive enough to incorporate into policy drafts. While not everyone was thrilled, the process yielded a more balanced outcome than a top-down edict would have.

Outside the forum, I continued my quiet moral mentorship. Younger colleagues at the social enterprise sought my advice on new challenges: balancing donor demands with community empowerment, integrating digital tools ethically, or navigating tensions between staff members of different cultural backgrounds. My counsel always returned to fundamentals: listening, empathy, honest reflection, and willingness to adapt.

In the neighborhood, the tradition of cultural evenings and mutual support continued. New families arrived from different corners of the country and even abroad, bringing fresh languages and customs. Instead of seeing these differences as threats, neighbors remembered how moral dialogues opened minds. We hosted a "Global Stories Night," where each household shared something unique from their heritage. Conflicts still arose, but moral reasoning had become a kind of social muscle memory. People knew they could address frictions by talking rather than withdrawing.

My grandchildren surprised me one day by announcing they'd formed a small discussion group at their school, inspired partly by what they'd seen at the forum. They wanted to tackle ethical dilemmas in their generation: data privacy on social media, bullying, climate activism in the face of adult indifference. I listened with pride as they described their sessions, how they encouraged classmates to speak honestly, how they learned to appreciate multiple perspectives. This was the legacy I yearned for: moral inquiry living on in young voices, evolving with new challenges.

I realized that while I had institutionalized moral reasoning in the forum and taught it to peers and youth, I could also connect with other cities or regions seeking similar methods. Modern communication technologies allowed video conferences and online workshops. I began collaborating with colleagues in distant places who wanted to replicate the Moral Inquiry Forum model. We shared guidelines, case studies, and success stories. Sometimes I led virtual training sessions, speaking to small communities hundreds of miles away, encouraging them to form their own moral circles and adapt the practice to their local contexts.

This network of moral inquiry efforts confirmed that we were seeding a movement, not just a single event. While I never sought grand recognition, I took comfort in knowing that others found value in these methods. Moral reasoning, once a personal struggle, had grown into a collective asset, a tool for civic renewal and ethical problem-solving.

Late one afternoon, I returned to the place where it had all started: my old school building. It had changed over the decades—new paint, additional classrooms—but I recognized the hallway where I once stood as a child, too afraid to speak. Now, as an elder, I strolled along these corridors, remembering how fear once felt overwhelming and how moral silence had isolated me. Standing there, I whispered thanks to those who, over my lifetime, invited me to speak, reason, and learn. Without their encouragement, I might never have discovered the transformative power of moral dialogue.

As I wandered outside, I noticed a group of students sitting under a tree—perhaps the successor to the old peepal tree gatherings. They chatted animatedly, passing around a short story they were analyzing. I caught fragments: they debated fairness, questioned how the story's characters treated each other, and seemed to enjoy dissecting moral nuances. I smiled, grateful that younger generations carried forward the tradition spontaneously, reminding me that moral inquiry needed no single founder or leader. It spread through inspiration and practice, each generation reinventing it for their time.

Approaching my twilight years, I contemplated my own mortality. Though healthy for my age, I knew my time was finite. The thought of leaving this world concerned me less now because I saw morality's continuity. Even if I vanished tomorrow, the forum would remain, colleagues would continue dialogues, my children and grandchildren would apply moral reasoning, and communities across the region would keep refining the practice. The tapestry extended far beyond my thread.

One last major challenge arose, as if to test the durability of our moral infrastructure. A sudden economic downturn hit the region—an unforeseen consequence of global markets shifting. Unemployment spiked, and once more, people argued fiercely about where to cut budgets, whom to prioritize, and how to prevent social unrest. Poverty lines deepened. Some advocated austerity measures that would harm the poor; others demanded wealth redistribution that frightened investors. Misinformation and suspicion spread like wildfire on social media.

The Moral Inquiry Forum responded swiftly. We convened emergency sessions, inviting economists, social workers, labor representatives, and business owners. We approached the crisis as we had the drought and the infrastructure debate: naming common values, telling human stories, exploring trade-offs. While the discussions didn't magically fix the economy, they prevented the moral discourse from collapsing into anger. By acknowledging everyone's fears, we found balanced policies: temporary safety nets for the unemployed, incentives for ethical business investments, educational initiatives to reskill workers for emerging sectors. Again, moral reasoning guided a fragile navigation, softening the impact of hard choices.

Seeing these results reassured me. Even under severe stress, our moral inquiry methods allowed for more humane governance and community solidarity. Moral reasoning had matured into a cultural resource. It didn't eliminate hardship, but it helped people face hardships together, reducing cruelty and despair.

As I celebrated a birthday—one of those milestones that remind you life is finite—my family and a few close colleagues gathered in our home. We shared a meal, reminisced about old times, and speculated about the future. My grandchildren brought friends, who greeted me respectfully but also curiously, as if sensing my role in shaping moral traditions they now took for granted.

Toward the evening's end, my eldest grandchild spoke up: "Grandpa, we've been discussing among ourselves how to improve our school's moral dialogues. We want more structure, maybe a set of principles like your forum uses. Could you help us formulate a small guide?"

My heart warmed. This was the perfect culmination. "Of course," I said, "but remember, it's your generation's turn to adapt these principles. I can share what worked for us, but you must shape it for your context."

They nodded seriously, understanding that moral reasoning must remain dynamic. Over the following weeks, we crafted a short guide: "Engaging in Moral Dialogue: A Youth Handbook." We kept it simple—tips on active listening, acknowledging complexity, treating disagreements as opportunities to learn, and remembering that empathy is key. My grandchildren shared it with their classmates, who welcomed the clarity. Soon, small moral circles sprouted in their school, tackling issues I could never have imagined: digital identity theft, AI-driven educational tools, and global youth activism for climate justice.

Watching this new wave of moral inquiry flourish, I realized I was witnessing a long lineage of moral dialogues unfolding through time. My life's work had been one link in a chain stretching backward and forward, each generation inheriting and refining the art of moral reasoning. In that chain, no single link was all-powerful, but together they formed a resilient tradition.

As my energy waned with age, I spent more time writing reflections and meeting with people who sought my counsel. Some wanted to replicate the Moral Inquiry Forum in distant cities. Others asked philosophical questions about whether morality could transcend cultural differences. I answered as best I could: yes, while moral reasoning always adapts to local contexts, certain principles—listening, empathy, honesty, humility—have universal relevance. And I emphasized that moral inquiry is not about imposing uniformity but enabling constructive engagement with differences.

In my final years, I felt a gentle peace. The world remained complex, with crises sure to come. But morality, as a living practice, had spread into various corners of society: schools, workplaces, communities, policy debates. People had learned to ask moral questions openly, not just resorting to force or despair. Moral reasoning had become a form of civic courage and collective intelligence.

Sometimes I sat alone under a tree—perhaps a descendant of the old banyan or peepal—and closed my eyes. I remembered my younger self, trembling with fear, unsure how to say "I'm afraid" or "I disagree." I recalled how moral inquiry began as small gatherings, how it guided me through personal choices, then scaled to workplace challenges, community building, and even large-scale crises. I smiled, knowing that fear had transformed into confidence, and silence into dialogue.

If I had one regret, it was that I never found a final, perfect moral formula. But I realized long ago that perfection was never the goal. The goal was to keep learning, keep talking, keep evolving ethically. Morality was a direction, not a destination—a horizon we approached by walking together, each step informed by reason, compassion, and respectful debate.

As word spread that I was writing my last essay, colleagues and friends asked for a "moral manifesto" summarizing what I learned. I chuckled at the grand term "manifesto," but agreed to write something down. In it, I stated:

- Morality thrives in relationships and dialogue.
- Complexity is natural; embrace it rather than denying it.
- Empathy, honesty, and humility are non-negotiable tools.
- Moral inquiry is a lifelong discipline, not a one-time lesson.
- No perfect solutions exist, but better solutions can be found through collective reasoning.

- Intergenerational exchange ensures moral inquiry's evolution.
- Implementing moral reflection in real contexts—policy, community action, personal life—makes moral reasoning more than theory; it becomes cultural practice.

I printed a few copies, but mostly shared it digitally. Many responded positively, some critiqued parts, and I welcomed their critiques as signs that moral dialogue would continue without me. Even as an elder, I learned from their feedback—proof that moral growth never ceases.

Eventually, my health began to decline. Nothing dramatic, just the slow fading common in old age. On a warm evening, my family gathered in my home. My partner held my hand, children and grandchildren sat close, friends and colleagues sent messages. I felt content, knowing the moral tapestry stretched far beyond my grasp. The world outside hummed with activity, but also, I believed, carried a deeper moral resonance than when I was young.

My grandchildren mentioned their latest moral circle discussion at school—the topic was balancing privacy rights with security measures. They said they'd managed a fair consensus, ensuring all voices were heard. I smiled, proud that the baton had truly passed on.

As I drifted toward sleep, I envisioned the tapestry again: countless threads woven by countless hands, each moral conversation adding texture and hue. I might slip quietly from this life, but moral reasoning, that precious art, would remain a living tradition—changing, adapting, guiding. The fear that once silenced me had long ago turned into a gentle courage that had spread through communities and generations.

In that final understanding, I let go, confident that whatever tomorrow brought—new crises, new dilemmas—someone would gather people in a circle, ask honest questions, listen deeply, seek shared values, and walk together toward solutions that honored human dignity and the planet's future. Moral reasoning would not vanish; it had become part of the world's ethical fabric, woven irrevocably into the tapestry of daily life.

I closed my eyes, hearing distant laughter, snippets of moral debate, the rustle of leaves under a tree, and the quiet murmur of voices continuing the work we had begun. It was enough, more than enough.

12

The Tapestry Unfurls Beyond a Lifetime

A gentle afternoon light filtered into the Moral Inquiry Forum's hall, illuminating the wooden floor and the circle of chairs where so many voices had shared their truths. People arrived quietly, some wearing thoughtful expressions, others with eyes that glistened. Word had spread that the founding elder, the one who had guided so many moral conversations across decades, had passed away peacefully in the early hours of the morning. The city seemed to move more slowly today, as if pausing to acknowledge the absence of a voice that had long helped it find its moral footing.

Among the arriving crowd were many familiar figures: colleagues who had shaped policy with careful moral reasoning, neighbors who had learned to welcome difference through cultural exchanges, younger activists who had debated infrastructure projects and equitable development. Students who had formed small reading groups in their schools came timidly, unsure if they belonged in the same room as seasoned advocates and elders. But here, everyone belonged. The forum's principle—everyone's perspective matters—remained intact.

Chairs filled, forming a loose, imperfect circle. At the center, a small table held a single candle, flickering softly. There was no formal leader now; the forum had never relied on a single authority. Someone cleared their throat, and a hush fell over the gathered assembly. They had come to remember, to reflect, and to consider how to carry the tradition forward now that its gentle architect was gone.

A longtime associate of the protagonist spoke first. He was older now, hair thinning, voice resonant with memory. "We are here," he said, "because the person who showed us how to listen, how to reason morally, and how to hold complexity with compassion, has departed." His words caught in his throat, but he continued: "Yet we know their legacy is not tied to a single life. They spent decades ensuring moral inquiry became a communal skill, not a personal gift."

Heads nodded. Across the circle sat a young woman who remembered attending her first forum session as a teenager, decades after the protagonist had begun their work. She spoke next: "I never knew them personally, only through these gatherings and stories. But I learned here that moral reasoning is something we practice together, over time. The structures they created—this forum, the guidelines, the spirit of dialogue—will outlast any one of us. Isn't that what they wanted?"

Murmurs of agreement spread. Another voice, from a representative who had once clashed fiercely during the infrastructure debates, said softly, "I remember how angry I was when I first came to these sessions. But by talking here, I realized no one was my enemy, only partners in finding better solutions. That lesson saved my community from a bitter fight. I owe that understanding to the moral methods passed down here."

As if prompted by an invisible hand, someone approached the small table at the center of the circle. They carried a folder—old pages, carefully preserved. "Before leaving us, the elder wrote a final letter," they said, voice trembling slightly. "It was found in their home this morning." The crowd inhaled quietly. This was a final gift from the one who had dedicated their life to moral inquiry.

Unfolding the letter with care, the reader began:

"To all who continue this work,

By the time you read these words, I will have stepped beyond this life's boundaries. I leave without regrets, knowing the moral tapestry we wove together is strong enough to endure. I have seen you apply moral reasoning to crises large and small, personal and communal. I have seen you refine these practices, teach them to children, adapt them to new challenges.

Remember, morality never depended on me alone. It thrives in your willingness to listen, to empathize, to acknowledge complexity without surrendering to hopelessness. Each of you carries forward the torch of moral inquiry. Just as I once stood timid and unsure, and later learned to speak and guide, so you too will evolve in your roles—some as quiet anchors, others as vocal facilitators, still others as researchers who deepen our ethical insights.

Pass these skills to future generations. Let children and youth see that confusion need not paralyze them, that disagreements need not breed hatred. Show them that by talking openly, acknowledging fears, and searching patiently for shared values, we can prevent despair and build communities rooted in respect and care.

I have no grand final words of moral law—only the reminder that moral reasoning is a living tradition. Keep it alive by practicing it daily, in your homes, workplaces, streets, and policymaking halls. Adapt it to technologies and new cultural dynamics, for the world will change again and again.

When you face new dilemmas—and you will—recall that we never found perfect answers, only better ways of approaching problems. That is enough. Better ways lead to less harm, greater fairness, deeper understanding. This is what moral growth means: not reaching a final summit but continuously climbing, together.

I leave you with gratitude for all we achieved. You have all contributed threads to this tapestry, ensuring its beauty. May it keep expanding, guided by the gentle art of moral inquiry.

Yours, always in spirit."

The reading ended, and silence held the room. Some wiped tears, others bowed their heads, absorbing the final message. It was, in essence, the elder's lifelong philosophy distilled: no final formula, no rigid doctrine, just a call to continue evolving morality as a shared craft.

After a pause, an older neighbor who had known the protagonist from their neighborhood days spoke: "They always told me moral reasoning was never a one-person show. Today proves that. Look around—this room is full of people ready to carry on. We have the memory of their teachings, and we have each other."

A middle-aged activist, once a staunch opponent of certain policies, now a calm mediator, added, "I realize I stand here not as a leader, but as a participant, just like everyone else. That's the legacy: no one dominates moral discourse; we all shape it."

A younger voice—perhaps a student—said, "I'm grateful I got to see them once. They visited our school's moral circle and encouraged us to find our own methods. Now, I want to share what I learned with my younger siblings and friends who struggle with online ethics and cultural tensions. We can keep adapting these principles to our new worlds."

As the circle absorbed these reflections, it became clear that the protagonist's departure did not leave a void of confusion. Instead, it revealed a garden of possibilities. Moral reasoning had become an ecosystem with many gardeners, each tending their patch, each planting new seeds of dialogue in their communities.

In the following days and weeks, the Moral Inquiry Forum continued its sessions, dedicating one meeting to planning how to extend its reach. Some members proposed regular workshops in schools and colleges, others suggested using digital platforms to connect with distant communities seeking moral guidance. A few volunteered to write updated versions of the moral inquiry guidelines, integrating lessons learned from recent crises and emerging technologies. Instead of a single figure guiding them, they formed a rotating facilitation team, ensuring that the responsibility for moral dialogue was shared among many.

In the neighborhood where the protagonist had lived, a small memorial garden was established. Instead of a statue or plaque extolling personal achievements, they planted a circle of saplings—one tree for each core value the forum had nurtured: empathy, humility, honesty, complexity, shared growth. The trees would grow over the years, offering shade to future generations who might sit under them and hold moral conversations, just as previous generations did under old trees decades ago.

Their children and grandchildren found comfort in these developments. They had worried that without the guiding elder, moral reasoning might falter. Instead, they saw that the community had internalized the art of inquiry so deeply that it no longer required a single mentor. The family, too, adapted, sharing memories and re-reading old notes from the elder. They laughed, recalling how once their grandfather or grandmother had gently corrected them or asked them to consider another perspective. Now they would do the same for each other and for younger relatives not yet born.

A few months later, a new moral challenge emerged—some emerging technology caused social upheaval, or a sudden environmental policy decision sparked debate. This time, no one panicked or doubted the process. They convened at the forum, invited stakeholders, shared personal stories, identified core values, explored nuanced solutions. The elder's method had become their method, seamlessly applied to fresh problems.

Seeing this continuity affirmed that the protagonist's vision for moral reasoning as a living, evolving practice had succeeded. Even in absence, their presence lingered in the way people listened before judging, asked questions instead of hurling accusations, and committed to long-term well-being over short-term gain. This living tradition outshone any memorial statue or official tribute.

Distant communities, hearing of this model's success, asked for guidance. The forum members, once novices, now provided mentorship to others. They ran remote sessions, advised on starting moral circles elsewhere, and wrote articles detailing how to handle complex ethical dilemmas through dialogue. Thus, moral reasoning expanded regionally and even internationally, a ripple effect from seeds planted long ago.

And so, the tapestry of moral inquiry continued to unfurl. Each new thread—be it a young student's question, a politician's willingness to consult communities, a neighborhood's resolve to welcome newcomers—wove into the pattern. The tapestry's colors shifted with time, reflecting changes in cultural norms, technologies, and global challenges. Yet the fundamental weaving technique—patient moral reasoning—remained.

Without fanfare, the elder's story concluded not at their passing, but in the lives and actions of countless others now practicing moral inquiry as a normal part of communal life. The protagonist's legacy lay not in achievements alone, but in the flourishing of a method that anyone could wield, the democratization of moral discourse that empowered individuals and groups to tackle complexity without losing hope.

One evening, a small group of youth gathered under a familiar tree—descendants of old peepal and banyan sessions. They discussed a new dilemma affecting their generation. Perhaps it was about balancing online communities with real-world responsibilities, or navigating a surge of misinformation. They listened, challenged each other, searched for shared values, and proposed creative compromises. None of them had met the original elder, yet all benefited from the moral tradition that person had helped establish.

As stars emerged above, one of them looked up and said, "We're lucky people before us took the time to learn how to talk, listen, and reason together. We might not always find perfect answers, but at least we know how to try."

A friend replied, "Isn't that the whole point? They taught us that trying, learning, and adapting morally is a never-ending journey. And we get to continue it."

In these words, the circle of moral reasoning completed another cycle. The elder's influence extended through time, from the seeds of their earliest courageous conversations to the robust forest of moral inquiry cultivated by countless minds and hearts. This was the true measure of their legacy: that moral reasoning became woven so tightly into daily life that no single thread's absence could unravel it.

As dawn approached on another day, life in the city and region continued—facing problems, celebrating joys, enduring setbacks, and striving for ethical solutions. Moral reasoning remained an ever-present companion, inviting each generation to refine, reinterpret, and improve their collective moral tapestry. The protagonist's chapter ended not in silence or despair, but in the ongoing music of voices reasoning together, ensuring that humanity's moral journey would forever move forward.

Epilogue

Many years later, the world looks both familiar and foreign to new generations who navigate its challenges with their own tools and tastes. They face moral dilemmas shaped by technologies we never imagined, cultural blends we never fully understood, and environmental shifts more intense than our forebears predicted. Yet, amid these uncertainties, a quiet strength endures: the tradition of moral inquiry passed down through time.

They may not know the names of those who, decades ago, first convened under old trees, who broke silences and asked careful questions. They may not recall each crisis that sparked honest debate, or the moment when moral reasoning blossomed into a community resource. But they feel the imprint of that inheritance whenever they pause to listen before judging, to consider consequences before acting, and to find shared values even in disagreements.

In busy city squares, classrooms, policy halls, and neighborhood gatherings, people continue to gather in circles—some small and intimate, others large and diverse—to unravel the threads of complex issues. They carry forward the core principles of dialogue, empathy, and honesty, adapting them gracefully to new contexts. Moral reasoning no longer depends on a single leader or generation; it thrives as a living tapestry, woven and re-woven by countless hands.

The seeds planted by those who learned to speak out when fear urged silence, who dared to question when conformity tempted complacency, have become forests of thoughtful voices. These voices, old and young, near and far, enrich public life with ethical nuance. The art of moral inquiry, once a fragile experiment, stands now as a quiet, resilient tradition guiding choices large and small.

As the world turns and new moral horizons appear, the legacy holds true: we may never find perfect answers, but through reasoned dialogue and shared understanding, we will always find better ways to live together.

References and Resources

Chapter 1: A House Full of Echoes

1. Bowlby, J. (1988). A Secure Base: Parent-Child Attachment and Healthy Human Development. New York: Basic Books.
2. Freud, S. (1905). Three Essays on the Theory of Sexuality. London: Hogarth Press.
3. Klee, M. (2015). "The Impact of Early Childhood Trauma on Development," Psychology Today.
4. Perry, B. D., & Szalavitz, M. (2006). The Boy Who Was Raised as a Dog. New York: Basic Books.
5. Erikson, E. H. (1963). Childhood and Society. W.W. Norton & Company.

Chapter 2: Unsteady Foundations

1. Bronfenbrenner, U. (1979). The Ecology of Human Development: Experiments by Nature and Design. Harvard University Press.
2. Winnicott, D. W. (1965). The Maturational Processes and the Facilitating Environment. New York: International Universities Press.
3. Anda, R. F., & Felitti, V. J. (1998). "The Adverse Childhood Experiences (ACE) Study," American Journal of Preventive Medicine.
4. Garbarino, J. (1999). Lost Boys: Why Our Sons Turn Violent and How We Can Save Them. New York: Free Press.

5. Vygotsky, L. S. (1978). Mind in Society: The Development of Higher Psychological Processes. Harvard University Press.

Chapter 3: A World Without Anchors

1. Piaget, J. (1950). The Psychology of Intelligence. Routledge.
2. Bandura, A. (1977). Social Learning Theory. Prentice-Hall.
3. Goffman, E. (1959). The Presentation of Self in Everyday Life. Doubleday.
4. Finkelhor, D. (2008). Childhood Victimization: Violence, Crime, and Abuse in the Lives of Young People. Oxford University Press.
5. Csikszentmihalyi, M. (1990). Flow: The Psychology of Optimal Experience. Harper & Row.

Chapter 4: Small Steps Toward the Light

1. Maslow, A. H. (1943). "A Theory of Human Motivation," Psychological Review.
2. Seligman, M. E. P. (2002). Authentic Happiness. Free Press.
3. Rogers, C. R. (1961). On Becoming a Person. Houghton Mifflin Harcourt.
4. Haidt, J. (2006). The Happiness Hypothesis: Finding Modern Truth in Ancient Wisdom. Basic Books.
5. Sapolsky, R. M. (2004). Why Zebras Don't Get Ulcers. Holt Paperbacks.

Chapter 5: Shaping a Voice of My Own

1. Arendt, H. (1958). The Human Condition. University of Chicago Press.
2. Krishnamurti, J. (1954). Think on These Things. HarperCollins.

3. Kohlberg, L. (1981). Essays on Moral Development, Volume I: The Philosophy of Moral Development. Harper & Row.
4. Freire, P. (1970). Pedagogy of the Oppressed. Continuum.
5. Nussbaum, M. C. (1997). Cultivating Humanity: A Classical Defense of Reform in Liberal Education. Harvard University Press.

Chapter 6: Embracing the Wider Horizon

1. Sen, A. (1999). Development as Freedom. Oxford University Press.
2. Habermas, J. (1984). The Theory of Communicative Action. Beacon Press.
3. Gandhi, M. K. (1940). The Story of My Experiments with Truth. Beacon Press.
4. Foucault, M. (1977). Discipline and Punish: The Birth of the Prison. Pantheon Books.
5. Sinek, S. (2009). Start with Why: How Great Leaders Inspire Everyone to Take Action. Portfolio.

Chapter 7: Walking Into the Wider World

1. Pinker, S. (2011). The Better Angels of Our Nature: Why Violence Has Declined. Viking.
2. Putnam, R. D. (2000). Bowling Alone: The Collapse and Revival of American Community. Simon & Schuster.
3. Rifkin, J. (2009). The Empathic Civilization: The Race to Global Consciousness in a World in Crisis. TarcherPerigee.
4. Tversky, A., & Kahneman, D. (1974). "Judgment under Uncertainty: Heuristics and Biases," Science.
5. Diamond, J. (1997). Guns, Germs, and Steel: The Fates of Human

Societies. W.W. Norton & Company.

Chapter 8: Expanding the Circle of Influence

1. Rawls, J. (1971). A Theory of Justice. Harvard University Press.
2. Appiah, K. A. (2006). Cosmopolitanism: Ethics in a World of Strangers. W.W. Norton & Company.
3. Harari, Y. N. (2015). Homo Deus: A Brief History of Tomorrow. Harper.
4. Sen, A. (2006). Identity and Violence: The Illusion of Destiny. W.W. Norton & Company.
5. Singer, P. (2009). The Life You Can Save. Random House.

Chapter 9: Weaving Morality into the Tapestry of Daily Life

1. Haidt, J. (2012). The Righteous Mind: Why Good People Are Divided by Politics and Religion. Pantheon Books.
2. Ostrom, E. (1990). Governing the Commons: The Evolution of Institutions for Collective Action. Cambridge University Press.
3. Elinor, E., et al. (2007). "Social Capital in Development Theory," World Development Report.
4. Sandel, M. J. (2009). Justice: What's the Right Thing to Do?. Farrar, Straus and Giroux.
5. Spivak, G. C. (1988). "Can the Subaltern Speak?" Marxism and the Interpretation of Culture.

Chapter 10: Passing the Torch of Moral Reasoning

1. Bloom, P. (2013). Just Babies: The Origins of Good and Evil. Crown.
2. Dewey, J. (1938). Experience and Education. Kappa Delta Pi.

3. Kegan, R. (1982). The Evolving Self: Problem and Process in Human Development. Harvard University Press.
4. MacIntyre, A. (1981). After Virtue: A Study in Moral Theory. University of Notre Dame Press.
5. Goleman, D. (1995). Emotional Intelligence: Why It Can Matter More Than IQ. Bantam Books.

Chapter 11: A Legacy of Moral Inquiry

1. Etzioni, A. (1993). The Spirit of Community: Rights, Responsibilities, and the Communitarian Agenda. Crown.
2. Wilkinson, R., & Pickett, K. (2009). The Spirit Level: Why More Equal Societies Almost Always Do Better. Allen Lane.
3. Rorty, R. (1999). Philosophy and Social Hope. Penguin Books.
4. Nozick, R. (1974). Anarchy, State, and Utopia. Basic Books.
5. Wright, R. (2000). Nonzero: The Logic of Human Destiny. Vintage.

Chapter 12: The Tapestry Unfurls Beyond a Lifetime

1. Harari, Y. N. (2014). Sapiens: A Brief History of Humankind. Harper.
2. Klein, N. (2014). This Changes Everything: Capitalism vs. the Climate. Simon & Schuster.
3. Rifkin, J. (2014). The Zero Marginal Cost Society. Palgrave Macmillan.
4. Zimbardo, P. (2007). The Lucifer Effect: Understanding How Good People Turn Evil. Random House.
5. MacKenzie, D. (2010). The Ethics of Influence: Government in the Age of Behavioral Science. Princeton University Press.

Behind the Dialogue

Thrinadh Sai is a captivating figure whose life is a testament to the transformative power of literature, philosophy, and an unrelenting pursuit of knowledge. Born in 1999 in the vibrant coastal city of Visakhapatnam, India, Thrinadh's journey is one of profound introspection, marked by both formidable challenges and inspiring triumphs. His life experiences shaped him into a deeply insightful author and thinker, whose works resonate with the complexities of the human spirit.

At the tender age of seven, Thrinadh faced the devastating loss of his father, a tragedy that left an indelible mark on his young life. However, it was his mother's unwavering strength and his own innate curiosity that became his guiding lights. In the face of hardship, Thrinadh sought solace in the world of books, discovering an enduring connection to the written word and the transformative power of ideas.

A pivotal moment in his intellectual awakening came with Rabindranath Tagore's Gitanjali. Its timeless verses ignited a thirst for understanding and set Thrinadh on a lifelong journey of self-discovery. This profound encounter with Tagore's poetry became the cornerstone of his creative and philosophical exploration.

Over the years, Thrinadh immersed himself in the works of literary and philosophical luminaries, including Arundhati Roy, Shashi Tharoor, Osho, Sri Aurobindo, Shankaracharya, Ramana Maharshi, Swami Vivekananda, Rumi, and more. These towering figures became his virtual mentors, guiding him through the intricacies of the human condition and inspiring him to articulate his own reflections on life, society, and spirituality.

At just 17 years old, Thrinadh found his poetic voice with the publication of his debut book, Emblem. A heartfelt collection of poems, it resonated deeply with readers and affirmed his calling as a writer. Since then, Thrinadh has authored six books spanning diverse genres, including poetry, short stories, and explorations of politics, philosophy, and psychology. Each work reflects his intellectual curiosity and creative depth.

Among his notable works, The Illusion of Democracy offers a sharp critique of political systems that exploit the common man, revealing Thrinadh's unwavering commitment to social justice. In Insights into the Human Mind, he delves into the intricate relationship between consciousness, spirituality, and the human experience, showcasing his fascination with the mysteries of existence.

Thrinadh's intellectual pursuits extend beyond the written word. A dedicated student of philosophy, psychology, and spirituality, he draws wisdom from ancient texts such as the Upanishads and the Bhagavad Gita. The teachings of Ramana Maharshi, Shankaracharya, Jiddu Krishnamurti, and Osho have deeply influenced his worldview, shaping a rich tapestry of thought that informs both his life and his writing.

A profound admirer of the legendary Telugu poet Sirivennela Seetharama Sastry, Thrinadh considers him a guru. Sastry's poignant words and insightful reflections continue to inspire Thrinadh, guiding him through his creative and personal journey.

Through his works, Thrinadh Sai invites readers to question conventional narratives, explore the depths of their consciousness, and embrace the complexities of life. His writing is not just a reflection of his journey but an invitation for others to embark on their own paths of self-discovery and understanding. With an unwavering commitment to truth and justice, Thrinadh's life and work stand as a beacon of hope and transformation, encouraging us all to strive for a more thoughtful, compassionate, and just world.

About the Author

Thrinadh Sai is a writer and thinker whose life is a testament to resilience, self-discovery, and the transformative power of ideas. Born in 1999 in Visakhapatnam, India, he turned personal struggles into a lifelong quest for understanding through literature, philosophy, and psychology. Inspired by luminaries like Rabindranath Tagore, Swami Vivekananda, and Jiddu Krishnamurti, Thrinadh has authored six thought-provoking books exploring themes of human consciousness, social justice, and the complexities of the human experience. His works, such as *The Illusion of Democracy* and *Insights into the Human Mind,* invite readers to reflect deeply, question norms, and embrace the pursuit of wisdom.

You can connect with me on:

https://thrinadhsai.com/the-author-thrinadh-sai

https://www.facebook.com/share/18SATgAmTw/?mibextid=wwXIfr

www.ingramcontent.com/pod-product-compliance
Lightning Source LLC
LaVergne TN
LVHW091323150826
845673LV00006B/1745

* 9 7 9 8 8 9 6 7 3 0 9 8 9 *